Life IS A Gift

The Duke Ellington Orchestra

Life
IS A
Gift

THE ZEN OF BENNETT

Tony Bennett

Foreword by Mitch Albom

HARPER

NEW YORK · LONDON · TORONTO · SYDNEY

I would like to dedicate this book
to my wonderful family, my lovely wife,
Susan Benedetto, and to Robert Henri's
The Art Spirit.

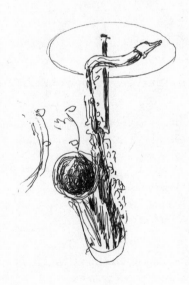

Musician, The Pearl Bailey Show

Contents

Contents

Foreword

BY MITCH ALBOM

We were standing on an empty concert stage. Tony Bennett opened his mouth.

"BUHP!"

The sweet, single note seemed to bounce off the rear wall and boomerang back to us, perfectly intact.

"Hear those acoustics?" he said.

"Do it again," I said.

"BUHP!"

He listened as the note resonated. Then he smiled, and I realized I was witnessing something rare: a man hearing the sound of his own voice and having every reason to delight in what he heard.

If there is, as the subtitle of this book suggests, a Zen of Tony Bennett, it is surely that: a philosophy of life so pure and honest that it can smile when it hears itself sung back. How many of us can say that? How many of us cringe at a recording of our own voices, or when we see ourselves on video, or when we think about how we acted yesterday or last year?

Tony Bennett, at eighty-six, can smile when his world is reflected—and with good reason. You are tempted to say talent, but many a talented artist has despised his own gifts. You are tempted to say success, but how many successful people are privately miserable?

No, the reason for Bennett's serene look—on that day in the concert hall, or any night he's onstage, or holding a brush in front of a canvas, or gazing out his window overlooking Central Park—is that he's doing what he wants to do, the way he wants to do it. He makes art. He makes friends. He gives away. He owns very little.

The word *Zen* is tied into enlightenment. First you seek it, then you share it.

The Zen of Tony Bennett is that he's still doing both.

———

Ask Tony about music, and he will quickly cite an influence—Art Tatum, his teachers after the war, his father, who once sang from a hilltop in an Italian village. Ask Tony about art, and he will defer to his instructors, or da Vinci, or any of the masters. Humble? This is a man who started his own arts high school, but named it after Frank Sinatra.

He shares credit. He deflects praise. The only thing he grips hard is his artistic standards. He became famous in a suit and never took it off, wore it through a hundred other fashions until it once again became the height of cool. He chooses tunes that are timeless, melodic, never consumed by the beat of the moment.

And because he sings the Great American Songbook, some might categorize Tony as conventional, but he has never been conventional, because conventional means you do anything to stay in vogue, you go from pop to rap, from writing to posting, from privacy to filming yourself on YouTube.

"Change or die," they say.

Or don't, Tony replies.

Now, *that's* Zen.

There is a reason Tony Bennett has won seventeen Grammys— the first in 1963, the latest forty-nine years later. It's because true art will stroke through fads and rise above the surface. It's the same reason both Bing Crosby and Judy Garland declared that Bennett was their favorite singer, but Amy Winehouse was thrilled to sing with him, too. The same reason he has won Emmy awards in two centuries. The same reason he's been welcome on *The Ed Sullivan Show* and *The Simpsons*.

Duke Ellington once said, "People do not retire. They are retired by others." Tony Bennett would not let that happen, and his perseverance has been rewarded and embraced. People sensed, correctly, that from decade to decade, he has remained true, a man who cares deeply about his art, and an artist who cares deeply about his humanity. His work on behalf of children, fellow musicians, and his hometown of Astoria, Queens, is inspiring. He does so many fund-raisers, he is jokingly nick-named "Tony Benefit."

Yet as you will see in these pages, his life has been full of its own poignant moments, holding his dying father's hand in a hospital, fighting in a war, lapsing briefly into drugs, hitting depression over a failing marriage, and having his spirits lifted by a choir in a hotel hallway, sent to him by Ellington himself.

Tony persevered and thrived, thanks mostly to his devotion to music. It has been his cape and his swaddling cloth, a gift to him and his gift to us.

"Go with truth and beauty, and forget everything else." It is one of the tips Bennett offers in this book, and part of why the *New York Times* recently said of Bennett's work, "We aren't likely to see a recording career like this again."

We aren't likely to see a man like this, either. I've been around so many people who meet Tony, and when they walk away say, "Gosh, I just want to hug him!"

I understand. He is the note that bounces off the wall and returns to you in gentle perfection. Who would ever want to let that go?

—Mitch Albom,
author of *Tuesdays with Morrie*
and *The Time Keeper*

Untitled

Musician (Bass)

How Do You Keep the Music Playing?

I've been performing professionally as an entertainer now for over sixty years. Somehow I can't believe the time has gone by so quickly. It's been an amazing journey, and I feel privileged that I've been successful doing what I love for my whole life. Of course there have been ups and downs, but I can honestly say that I have always tried to learn from my mistakes.

I rarely look back; instead, I always look forward. There is so much of life that we miss when we wallow in regret. My energy is better spent concentrating on all the things I have yet to learn and experience. I think this has made me into a much better person. I'm at peace with myself now, and I look forward to each new day.

———————

From a young age, I was taught never to compromise. My parents and teachers showed me that you should make every move with care, and put the accent on quality. If you apply this philosophy, you will never go wrong. And I have found that, in particular for a performer, the public will pick up on that attitude and will reward you by giving back what you give to them. I never sing a cheap song. I never look down at the audience and think that they are ignorant, or think that I'm more intelligent than they are. To think otherwise is totally incorrect, and runs contrary to everything I was raised to believe.

I love entertaining people; I strive to make them feel good, and they make me feel wonderful. To explain it simply, I love what I do, and my ambition is to get better as I get older. That's really what I'm all about.

To my mind, being in the entertainment business is the best job that anyone could have. I get to travel the world over, meet interesting people, and experience many cultures. I've become close to artists of all ages in music, art, and the theater. I've sung for eleven presidents, and have performed for royalty. But, best of all, I get to meet my fans—the people on the street—face-to-face. They are the ones who help me stay grounded. I learn more from them than from anyone else.

I'm also lucky because I get to work with my family. I'm blessed with creative children: my eldest son, Danny, has been my manager for over thirty years, and my son Daegal produces and engineers my records. My daughter Johanna has dedicated her life to philanthropic endeavors; my youngest, Antonia, is a talented singer in her own right and often joins me on tour. My wife, Susan, has worked with me in realizing my dream of establishing a New York City public high school for the arts, and she travels with me wherever I go. Being surrounded by family is very important to me. It's such a privilege to be able to do what I do.

From an early age, I've been blessed by knowing that I wanted to be involved in artistic endeavors. Even though we were very poor, my parents placed a high value on the arts. I always wanted to sing and paint; I never had to ask, "What am I going to do with my life?" I just knew.

I meet so many intelligent people who seem to know so much, but I often find that what they lack is an understanding of their innermost desires. They really have no idea what they want to do with their lives; they have no vision or sense of the bigger picture, and often they lack the passion that is essential to a truly fulfilled life. I guess I'm just lucky that way. I've always had this passion—this feeling that I have no choice but to do what I do. And fortunately I'm still in that state right now. I'm grateful that to this day, my passion and thirst for knowledge have continued.

My goal is to improve all the time. Here I am today, at eighty-six, and I'm even more passionate now than ever before. I'm at the top of my game, and things just keep getting better and better. I'm proud to say that I feel I've never worked a day in my life—and I know that's because I love what I do.

The Zen of Bennett

Work doesn't feel like work if you're passionate about what you do.

Do something to improve yourself, every single day.

Choose a career that encompasses what you gravitate to naturally, and you'll have a satisfying lifelong vocation.

San Francisco

Life IS A *Gift*

My Mom

Only Sing Good Songs

I grew up in an era when there was no such thing as planned obsolescence; instead, everything was made with quality. Like so many people my age who came out of the Great Depression, I grew up with a strong sense of appreciation for what little we had. My grandfather owned a grocery store, and my mom was a seamstress working under sweatshop conditions. But despite the harsh circumstances, they always took time to make the children in the family feel special. I never took for granted the importance of the love of my family and friends to pull me through hard times. They taught me humility, and instilled in me a work ethic that remains to this day.

I was drilled not to be the best, but to always strive to *do* my best—and that if I did, the rewards would follow. I was told that everything I do should be done with care. Even now, I feel strongly that if you buy a suit or a dress, it should be well made, and it should last for years—instead of a con job where you buy something only to have to replace it after it falls apart six months later. You can go broke that way. It makes better sense to save up your money to buy one well-made suit than ten cheap suits.

There should be a law against planned obsolescence, and everyone should follow this lead. In other words, an artist or a company, or an individual, should not put out a work of art, or a song, or any product that he knows won't endure.

When I was ten, my father passed away. After he died, my mother had to support the three of us kids all by herself. She did what they called "piecework," earning a penny per dress, sewing all day long in the factory. She'd bring work home with her every night. Once or twice in an evening, she'd come across a bad dress—one of such poor quality that she'd refuse to work on it. We were desperate for money, but she couldn't bring herself to do something she felt was beneath her. "I only do quality dresses," she would say. "I'm not going to work on a bad one." Many years later, I realized that this was the attitude I held toward my job, too. She became my inspiration for insisting on singing only quality songs.

Years later, another experience that reinforced this idea was my training at the American Theatre Wing on Forty-Fourth Street, which I attended after returning home from Germany after my service in World War II. The government had set up the GI Bill so that soldiers could receive an education. The bill paid tuition for either trade school or college and gave a lot of fellows like myself the chance to keep going with the education that the war had interrupted, and to attend a school we couldn't have afforded without it. People like Marlon Brando, Harry Belafonte, Paul Newman, Shelley Winters, and Sidney Poitier took classes there.

The Theatre Wing was a fantastic school, and my teacher had trained with Stanislavsky, who founded Method acting. I've applied the techniques I learned in that school to my singing ever since. I think of the lyrics in an autobiographical way, as if they were written about something I've lived through. Not every song allows for this; only the well-crafted ones do. So I make it a point to seek out quality songs that provide that kind of powerful emotion, and as a result, the public can experience them the way that I do. As they listen to me sing, they get an honest sense of how I'm feeling while I perform. This connection between singer and audience would be impossible if I added a cheap song to my repertoire, which is why I never have.

The Theatre Wing not only taught me the importance of doing quality work; my teachers there also told me not to listen to anyone who tried to tell us otherwise. I never really appreciated how valuable that attitude was until the producer Mitch Miller signed me to my first recording contract in 1950.

Mitch was the head of A&R—Artist & Repertoire—at Columbia, and his job was to sign new talent for the label. He was a great classical oboist who saw how much money novelty music was making, and he became the first producer to make a fortune doing commercial songs for the masses. From the moment they signed me, everyone at the company tried to change the way

I sang. They couldn't get over the fact that I loved jazz. Jazz wouldn't sell as well as pop, and they wanted to try to stop me from singing what I wanted to. All they thought about was how many albums they could sell to the public. When the record companies saw how much money they could make doing pop tunes, they started telling their artists what to do. They always thought they knew best, and they refused to trust the artists' own instincts. In the early years of the music business, things were different. Producers would just say, "Record a song for us," and the singer did what came naturally. But the times were changing.

I constantly went up against Mitch. Personally I liked him, but he preferred gimmicky music and very accessible songs, as opposed to tunes from the American Songbook. He came up with this concept for *Sing Along with Mitch*—a weekly TV show featuring a chorus of singers. The home audience sang along to the words shown on the screen, complete with a bouncing ball. It was a huge hit and made a lot of money for the company. In addition, he didn't have to deal with "temperamental artists" when he was doing that show.

Mitch really didn't like jazz. He didn't care for Duke or Count Basie—and when I came to the label, I was a jazz singer. He tried to have me sing sweet music that would be immediately forgotten, and novelty stuff that was silly, stupid, and ignorant. I would buck him and say, "No, I just want to sing quality songs."

I never did (and never will) do anything just to pick up the money and run, but sticking to my guns became quite a battle for me during the early years.

So I fought with Mitch over these ridiculous tunes that he wanted me to sing. To his credit, I did get a lot of hit records—"Because of You," "Cold, Cold Heart," "Blue Velvet"—although I was really careful about which of those songs I chose to do. But without fail, he would then insist that I record something trite while I was hot, instead of doing a classic song or a jazz number. I had to fight for every single one.

After a few years, when we both realized this back-and-forth would never end, Mitch and I finally worked out a compromise: for every two pop pieces I'd do for him, I would get to do two jazz songs. That worked for a while. Then, in what would become a big turning point in my creative career, for the first time in the history of the music industry, a lawyer named Clive Davis became the president of Columbia Records. This came as a shock to many of us, as we were used to artists such as songwriter Johnny Mercer, who founded Capitol Records, and Frank Sinatra, who started Reprise Records, running the business.

Clive's becoming president was the first step on the road to a corporate mentality in music making. In the sixties, when rock music became so prevalent, Clive tortured me to do an album covering contemporary songs. After a while, when I felt I had no choice, I actually got physically sick while recording that album; it never made any sense at all to me.

It seemed like the world was turning upside down. Everyone

was turning on and tuning out; it reached a point of absolute insanity. My favorite story of all time was the one about Duke Ellington, when he got let go from Columbia. Clive Davis asked Duke into his office one day. "Mr. Ellington, I have some bad news for you," he said. "We are going to have to drop you from the label."

"How come?" Duke asked. "Well, you're not selling enough records," Davis replied. Then Duke said, "I think you have it turned around. I thought *I* was supposed to make the records, and *you* were supposed to sell them."

The funny thing was that I was giving it my all for those guys; 100 percent of my creative effort. They just didn't seem to appreciate it. That's what happens when the bean counters take control—things go down the tubes. It's still happening today, but if everyone who holds the reins in this business would put their faith in the artists that they sign, things would be in a much better place. Movies and books need powerful stories, and great records need the best songs. If I really adore a song, I'm able to get into the creative zone and deliver the definitive version—one that conveys what the composer originally had in mind. That way, the public will know they're hearing the real thing, instead of some put-on. It's obvious when a record producer thinks that the public is stupid, because they'll try to dumb things down. But that type of work never endures.

I'm not saying I was the only one that this kind of thing happened to. Every artist has to deal with producers who know it all, and who just want to try to make a quick buck. Even the greats like Fats Waller, Nat King Cole, and Billie Holiday had to deal with it. I'll tell you another classic: Fats Waller was having a jam session up in Harlem, and he wrote "Ain't Misbehavin'" on the back of a paper bag. The record company paid him two bottles of gin for that song. Every artist who performed popular music sang it, and it became a huge Broadway smash that eventually toured the world. The label made millions and millions of dollars from that one song, and he got paid two bottles of gin. That's just a sin.

By bucking the advice of Mitch Miller and Clive Davis, and sticking with the good songs, I've been able to have top-selling records with every generation from the fifties until now. I have been privileged not only to contribute many hit songs to the American Songbook but to have a catalog that I can be proud of. There isn't one record from 1950 until now that is dated. They're all done with the best composers, great musicians, and top engineers, and there isn't one that I'm embarrassed by.

Honing my performance and refusing to compromise have paid off for me, and now I've been discovered all over again by yet another generation. I recently released my complete collection boxed set that contains everything I've recorded. There are sixty-three albums, and there isn't one song where I thought, *I wish hadn't put that in there.*

Duke Ellington used to quote Toscanini, who said, "Music is either good, or it isn't. It's not someone's opinion." What he was saying is that there shouldn't be any categories in music; that's not what it's supposed to be about. Quality music will still be heard a hundred years from now, and still be relevant. The cream will rise to the top, and history will reveal those that endure. And that's where it's at.

I believe Toscanini's statement with all my heart, which is why I love to sing from the vast catalog of American music. In fact, in the sixties, Alec Wilder, renowned *New Yorker* music critic Whitney Balliett, and I did a radio show in which we were the first to articulate the importance of and coin the phrase "the Great American Songbook." I travel all over the world, and wherever I go, people know all those songs by heart. There isn't an instance that they don't start singing along with me. These tunes are so well known that they are our best ambassadors.

I compare this songwriting period that began in the 1920s to the time of the post-Impressionist painters, when a true renaissance in art was taking place in France. Those changes were happening not only in art but in music, too, with Debussy, Tchaikovsky, and Ravel. I regret that we don't have that kind of emphasis on quality nowadays. Instead, greed rules most of the industry. Often the music is intentionally disposable; it's forgotten two minutes after it comes out—whereas the songs that became the Great American Songbook will continue to endure.

During the recording of my last duets record, Willie Nelson and I discussed the fact that although he and I come from different places in the country, musically we are cut from the same cloth. Artists like Frank Sinatra and Ray Charles were on his radio or record player when he was growing up, because his parents and grandparents were musicians, and they listened to good music. Willie would sit at the piano stool with his guitar in hand while his sister played "Stardust" or "Moonlight in Vermont," and he'd learn them along with her. He says he got a fantastic education just listening to her play those tunes.

Frank Sinatra, Nat King Cole, and Ella Fitzgerald were ten years older than I was. They were the ones who inspired me to say, "Someday I'd like to be like that." Today you can listen to a Sinatra or Nat King Cole album, and it sounds like they recorded it yesterday. Nat singing "Lush Life" is just gorgeous, and the same holds true for Sinatra's "In the Wee Small Hours of the Morning." Their music will be appreciated until the end of time.

The public might get the impression that singers only want number-one hits, but that has never been my premise. Instead of being number one, I only wanted to be one of the best. I just keep being myself, and I never compromise. I never strived for a hit song, some novelty tune that would hit it big but be forgotten in two weeks; I wanted a hit catalog. If I do something, I want it to be top quality.

The Zen of Bennett

There should be no planned obsolescence; don't just pick up the money and run. Instead, create something of lasting quality and you will reap the rewards.

Despite what others say, refuse to compromise your high standards.

People will reward you if you consistently produce high-quality work.

Instead of focusing on being number one, attempt to be one of the best.

Ralph Sharon

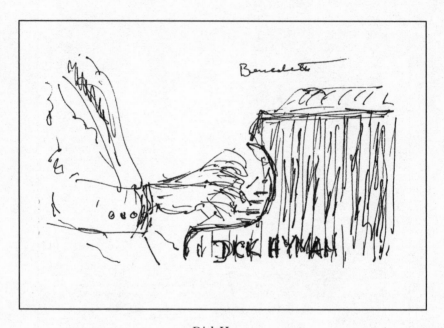

Dick Hyman

2

I've Always Been Unplugged

I started performing in 1950. I've seen the whole music business change, from recording in monaural to stereo, to quadraphonic to digital, but I've always loved recording to two-track tape. It sounds much warmer, and I like going for the warmth. It's very intimate, friendly, and simple; it doesn't sound metallic or electronic. I think tape captures what the ear hears more accurately than a digital recording does. Tape reproduces sound with feeling, as if it's being performed in a concert hall; for me, it's the most natural sound possible.

Technology took a big leap when the microphone was invented. Bing Crosby invented the art of "intimate singing," as he was able to hold a microphone up to his mouth and sing softly. It really made the public go crazy. The point is, he used the new technology in ways that brought out the best in his technique.

The important thing to understand is that technology can't guarantee you a good take, or transform a take that isn't good to one that's better. It all boils down to how you're singing that day, how much you've prepared, and how much talent you have to put into it. Sometimes we lose that notion, in this era of mixing and everyone recording single instruments in different rooms at different times. But it really isn't about the technology at all—it's all about the performance. That's why, when I won the Grammy for the *MTV Unplugged* album, I made it a point to remind the audience during my acceptance speech that "I've always been unplugged."

Years ago, artists and composers just wanted to capture a good, pure performance. I met Ira Gershwin once in my life, when I was at the Chappell Music offices. "Get that song for Mr. Bennett that I'm thinking of for him," Ira said to his assistant, Frank Military. So Frank ran off, and when he came back, he said, "Mr. Gershwin, we not only have the music, but we have a record of it. And it's in stereo!" Gershwin turned to him. "I don't need stereo," he said. "I have two ears." Instead of worrying about the recording technique, he just wanted a good performance from the artist. That was all that mattered.

A lot of performers like to show off, but it's not about how many notes you're playing; instead, it's how well you can construct a meaningful interpretation of a song. As far as I'm concerned, less is always more. My art teacher, Everett Kinstler, always reminds me that he doesn't like paintings where the artist used twenty-seven different colors. As he often says, "John

Singer Sargent used only six colors." By doing something in a minimal way, you can get closer to the feeling of it. You don't have to search for emotion; somehow it reveals itself when you keep it simple, and the work of art or the song ends up being soulful.

I insisted on recording all the duets albums live with my partners. This is not how albums are recorded today, but it keeps the performance vibrant. These days, most artists record all the instruments separately first, and add in the vocals later. But with jazz, everybody's in the room, and we just play spontaneously. What you hear on those CDs is exactly what we put on tape that day.

That's how I did all my recordings over the years—in the studio and live. My favorite studio was the CBS 30th Street Studio in New York. CBS converted a grand church into a recording space, because it had the most amazing acoustics. Artists from Toscanini to Duke Ellington to Bob Dylan made their best albums there. Sadly, CBS decided to sell the building, and it was torn down to make way for an apartment complex. (With its history, it should have been designated a landmark historic site and never touched. Corporate greed is everywhere we look, but we need to appreciate our American traditions and historic contributions in a much better way.)

Frank Laico, my recording engineer at 30th Street at the time, would set up the entire orchestra with my vocal mic placed right in the center so I could hear and feel every note. We would let the tape roll, and in one or two takes, we'd be done. We would complete a whole album's worth of material in two days, tops. That's why those records live and breathe to this day.

Most of the duet artists were shocked that we planned on recording everything in two or three takes—most artists might take twenty-five weeks to finish one record. But not all; Elton John sat down at the piano and did "Rags to Riches" in only one take. When the Dixie Chicks came in to sing "Lullaby of Broadway" with me, one of the band members, Emily Robison, wasn't used to the way I recorded, but when they got going, they sang so well that it felt so natural. It was the first time they'd done a swinging tune, and it wound up selling millions of records. They were very pleased with the way it came out.

Natalie Cole found the live work in the studio very different, too, but she really enjoyed it. She noted that because you can't keep the musicians there all day long while you figure out how to work the song, you really have to be on point with your material and do all of your preparation before getting to the studio, so you can hit the ground running. Josh Groban told me how much he enjoyed not having to worry about wearing earphones. It was a relief for him just being able to feel the energy and relative pitch in the room. Willie Nelson compared the way we taped the duets to working in a small club. He said he felt as if there were people sitting with a couple of drinks in front of them out there at the tables.

Overall, the reaction to recording live has been universally positive, despite the fact that nowadays everyone uses a very different method of laying down the material. I think it all comes back to the fact that you have to have a strong performance in order to get a good take. All the technology and mixing in the world can't create something if the talent isn't there in the first place.

The Zen of Bennett

If you win over the audience, then you've got it made—regardless of what management says.

You can't get a good take from technology, or transform a bad take into something that's good.

It all boils down to how you're singing that day, and your preparation for it.

Duke Ellington—Black Rain

3

Proper Involvement

As you can imagine, I've run across a great many people throughout my career—from fellow performers, actors, painters, world leaders, and presidents to royalty. Some were mere acquaintances; others professionals; others turned out to be lifelong friends. I can't stress enough the importance of friendships throughout my life. I have had so many wonderful relationships with all sorts of people—and, funny enough, the most enduring friendships I have to this day were with the kids I knew growing up in Astoria, Queens.

Over and over again, it's been made clear to me that you can't go it alone. No matter what obstacles I run up against, my friends have been indispensable, and have been there for me at every turn. In different ways, each one taught me how to be a better person, or how to become a better performer.

Some of my most lasting relationships, and people I've learned quite a bit from, came through the music business. Duke Ellington, who became a good friend of mine through the years, was one of those people. I idolized him, as did every other musician in the world at the time. Duke *was* the Jazz Age—and I learned so much from him.

Once, in the early days of my career, Duke and I were slated to do a live *Ed Sullivan Show* together. A few minutes before I was to go on the air, I went to stand by Duke, and he could see that I was nervous. He just put his hands on my shoulders and said, "Eliminate all negativity. Stress is a killer; just be positive." The lights went on and the cameras started rolling, and somehow we made it work. I never forgot his calming influence in that crucial moment, and that was the beginning of a long and fruitful collaboration.

Duke and I got to know each other well through playing a lot of gigs together, and eventually he embraced my whole family. He said that my mom was one of the most spiritual people he'd ever met, and his sister also became close with mine. It was what he would call "proper involvement"—a warm friendship based on mutual respect.

Once Duke and I happened to be staying at the same hotel in Boston. I was talking to my dear friend and jazz cornet player, Bobby Hackett, who had come to visit me. My phone rang, and it was Duke. "Come down to the ballroom in the lobby; I have a song for you," he said. So Bobby and I went down in the elevator to meet him.

Duke was already sitting at the piano, ready to play his new piece. But when he started to play, he realized that the middle octave of the piano was totally out of tune. That didn't stop him, though; he played the whole song for us without the middle eight notes! The music flowed out of his fingers for over an hour, and I was in seventh heaven. As for Bobby, tears were streaming down his face, he was so happy listening to those creative sounds. Nothing stopped Duke; whereas most people would get totally bugged, he just laughed it off and found his way around the bad notes. He kept everything positive—that was Duke.

When I celebrated my twentieth year in show business, I did a tour with Duke and his orchestra. Whenever I worked with Duke Ellington or Count Basie, I gave them top billing. Other people in the business had advised me never to do this, saying that I should always make sure my name was on top of the marquee. But my respect for them outdid showbiz politics. It gave me such pleasure to see their names headlined in the bright lights.

Duke and I played twenty-five concerts starting in New York City with the New York Philharmonic, continuing across the entire United States. My genius pianist at the time, Ralph Sharon, was a jazz composer, and he'd always wanted a chance to see Duke's music, so early one morning he went to the rehearsal room to have a look. He spent a while poking about, but he couldn't find one piece of written music lying around anywhere.

Later Ralph asked Harry Carney, Duke's baritone sax player, about it. "We don't use sheet music," Harry said. "We know our parts." Ralph was shocked. When Duke wrote a new piece, the band would learn it entirely by heart. Duke would play it for them a few times, and they would just pick it up. They were performing the most complicated music ever, and they were learning it all by memory. Ralph and I were in awe of the level of musicianship and sheer brilliance of Duke and the members of his band; it set a high standard of excellence that raised the bar for all of us.

Duke also had a habit of making sure we kept in touch. He was as creative in that department as in everything else he did. Every time he wrote a new song, he would send me a dozen roses; it was a little tradition he began. A bunch of flowers would arrive at my house, and I'd say, "Duke's been at it again."

I was always incredibly flattered that he would make this thoughtful gesture for me. That's why, on the occasion when I painted Duke's portrait, in tribute to his generosity, I painted roses into the background. Of all the portraits I've painted, Duke's is my absolute favorite; I was inspired by the peaceful expression on his face, and that is why I inscribed it with the words "God Is Love." It now hangs in the National Portrait Gallery in the Smithsonian. Whenever I see it, it reminds me of this beautiful man and the legacy of amazing music that he gave to the world.

I was presented with another opportunity to honor Duke on his seventy-second birthday, which we celebrated in New York at the Waldorf-Astoria. I sang some songs to him as he was sitting in the audience, and he came up and played several numbers. Then I brought out a cake and everyone in the crowd sang "Happy Birthday" to him. It was a moment I will always remember.

When I lived in Los Angeles, I made a number of good friends in the entertainment business, all of whom came to my fiftieth birthday party. I was in my backyard taking in the crowd and chatting with my friend Johnny Carson—I'd known him ever since I was the first guest, along with Groucho Marx, to appear on his show—when Johnny noticed Fred Astaire and Cary Grant standing by the pool with their sleeves rolled up, laughing together about something. "Look, Tony; you can't beat that image of those two standing next to one another," Johnny said. "Everyone in the business is here." I could have pinched myself. It's hard to describe the quiet pride I felt in having earned the friendship of these legendary figures.

Astaire lived near me when I had my home in L.A. He used to stop in at my little art studio, which was right by my swimming pool. In it, I had a radio and my easel, and Fred liked to spend time with me there. One day he came over to relax, but I could tell something was on his mind. "I love to go to parties," he said. "But all the women want me to dance with them. I'm no longer an athlete, though. I don't know what to say to them, and I don't want to be rude, so I wind up having to leave early. It really bothers me."

I commiserated with him for a minute, and then Astaire commented on how much he liked the song playing on the radio; it was by Big Joe Turner, the blues singer. Then we started talking about my new material. "Where's that song you're working on?" he asked. It was up in my bedroom, and he asked me to go up and get it so he could listen to it.

As I came back down to the studio, I happened to glance into the pool house window. There was Astaire, dancing just as he did in any one of his major films, to the tune on the radio. When I opened the door to the studio, he turned red in the face, and was so embarrassed that I'd caught him. "I can't help it, Tony," he said. "Whenever I hear the right beat, I just have to dance." Astaire got caught up in the music and was doing these moves that most twenty-year-olds couldn't pull off. That was one of the many instances in which it became clear to me that age really has nothing to do with anything; it's all about your attitude and your love for what you do. Astaire's energy and artistry will stay with me for the rest of my life.

———————

Cary Grant was another who gave me good advice at a time when I was at a crossroads in my career. After I had done my first film, Cary gave me some great insights. "When you make a movie, you have to spend all day waiting around in your trailer just preparing to act for fifteen minutes, and you don't get to spend time with people," Cary said. "Take it from me—it's no way to spend your life. Just keep performing and follow your passion, Tony. You love to sing and paint, so travel the world and be the best entertainer. You make people feel fantastic; you're alive." Cary's counsel to do what you love, and concentrate on what you know best, is something that all of us would do well to bear in mind.

Once Cary and I went to the racetrack together. It was quite an experience to be out in public with him; all the women would practically pass out as he walked by. The track was very well kept, and everything about it was top of the line. I said to Cary, "Boy, this is a great place. Do you come here often?" Cary said, "Yeah, I would hope so. I own the track."

———————

I learned many a valuable life lesson from my close friend Nat King Cole. The first time I ever heard Nat's voice was when I was a soldier stationed in Germany. I loved the way he revealed himself so honestly in his songs; he could sing like an angel. That's really the whole idea—to let the audience know how you truly feel—and Nat accomplished that every time he performed. In fact, his daughter Natalie, with whom I sang some of the duets, told me recently that she thought I was a lot like her father, and that was why Nat and I got along so well. She felt that we made similar choices when we performed, and she also said that we acted the same way offstage as we did onstage. To me, that was one of the best compliments I had ever received, because I believe in the importance of an authentic performance.

Back when I was an eighteen-year-old kid fighting in the trenches, I never would have guessed that I'd wind up getting to know one of my musical idols. But once I returned to the States and my singing career got going, eventually Nat and I wound up with the same agent. Finally we met in person in the agency's New York office.

We started talking, and I mentioned that I'd just come from seeing my mom in New Jersey. Nat asked me if I took a limousine. "I don't use a limo; I take the bus," I told him. Nat was shocked that while I had four hit records at the time, and was all over the charts, I still took a bus back from my mother's house. He seemed to appreciate the fact that I didn't put a lot of effort into acting like a big star. From that point on, we always got along extremely well. His approval reinforced my sense that keeping things simple and being humble about success were good qualities to strive for.

Nat did me a huge favor in the early days of my career. I was big in New York, but I hadn't made a dent in Chicago yet, although the city was an important venue for musicians at that time. Nat was supposed to do some shows in the Chez Paree nightclub there, but after he'd accepted the date, he was asked to perform at the White House and had to cancel. He suggested to the club's owners that they have me fill in for him. I was thrilled to do it, and the show went over really well. That was a wonderful break for me, and it was all due to Nat. His generosity inspired me to try to help other younger artists who are coming up in the music business. It's a tough industry to succeed in, and I like to think that I've followed Nat's example by giving a boost to those who are just starting out.

A funny thing happened at that first engagement in Chicago. Sophie Tucker was the headliner at the Chez Paree, but after I had been performing there for a month, my show was such a hit that the owners wanted to give me equal billing. We solved the problem by having SOPHIE TUCKER AND TONY BENNETT on one side of the marquee, and TONY BENNETT AND SOPHIE TUCKER on the other half of the sign. The club arranged to have Sophie's driver always bring her in from the direction that featured her name on the top, so she never saw the side with my name first.

Nat and I performed countless shows together over the years. Toward the end of his career, when he had a huge hit with "Rambling Rose," I found myself backstage at the Sands in Las Vegas, listening to him rehearse. "I'm going to walk through the audience while I do the song, and sing to people at each table," Nat explained to the manager. But the manager didn't want Nat leaving the stage. Suddenly there was a big conflict.

I remember thinking, *I'm not going to say a word; I'm just going to sit here and mind my own business.* But then the manager really scolded Nat. "Don't do that tonight. It's not going to work," he said. "You can't walk through the room; it's ridiculous to do that." But Nat, always one to stand up for his artistic vision, insisted, and they started to get into it.

At this point, I felt I had to jump in. From my seat backstage, I shouted, "Don't worry, Nat. You have the number-one song in the country—you can do whatever you want!" Even the manager had to laugh, and that broke the ice.

In the end, Nat got his way. I was there at his show when he walked from table to table and personally made everyone in the audience feel comfortable. It created such a warm atmosphere in the room, and it worked out beautifully. Nat knew exactly how to make his audiences happy, and he wasn't going to let some management type put a crimp in his style. I took note of his insistence on keeping it personal, and have tried to do the same ever since.

Later, after the show at the Sands, Nat told me that he wanted Ella, Count Basie, and me to perform with him in a new theater, the Dorothy Chandler Pavilion, which was opening in Los Angeles the following year. Of course I was thrilled to sing wherever Nat requested me to, and enthusiastically I agreed. But several weeks before the show was going to open, Dean Martin called to tell me that Nat was very ill with cancer. I was so sad when Nat died just a few days after Dean's call. I crushed my pack of cigarettes, threw them in the trash, and never went back to smoking again. Frank Sinatra took over the planning, and the performance became a memorial to Nat. I think he would have been very proud of it.

––––––––––

Sinatra was actually my best friend in show business. Despite his tough-guy persona, he was one of the most kindhearted people in a position of enormous power that I have ever met.

He encouraged me when I was new to the business, and as I'll describe in more detail later, in a high-profile interview he told the whole world that I was his favorite singer—a career-altering statement that even now I can't believe he made about me.

After fifteen years of performing, there were some people in the industry who still didn't take me seriously. But once Frank named me his favorite, his audiences began to listen to my music. To me, that was the height of true friendship and generosity, and also a confirmation of Frank's self-confidence—a rarity in our business. It showed me the importance of encouraging and promoting younger talents.

Frank's thoughtfulness has left a lasting impression on me. In the middle of one of his television specials in the mid-seventies, Frank stopped to tell the audience (and all the viewers watching at home), "Tony Bennett is my favorite guy in the whole world." This alone was incredible, but it was even more meaningful because Frank knew that my mother and I would be watching together at her home, and he also knew that my mom was very ill. Every time I went to visit her, I wondered if it would be the last time I'd ever see her. My mom's face lit up like a little child's when Frank said those words. It was such a warm gesture, particularly since Frank realized that it would mean so much to her.

Frank was always looking out for me. During one of his shows in L.A., I had snuck into the audience and was swooning along with all the girls. Right after he finished singing "How Do You Keep the Music Playing?" he stopped and looked my way. "Hey, Tony, you should do this song," he said. He blew me right out of my seat! I had no idea he realized I was in the audience. And, boy, if Frank told you to do something, you had better make sure you did it. But, kidding aside, I immediately worked that song into my repertoire. And do you know what? He was right—it was perfect for me. For many, it has become a highlight of my set, and one of my all-time favorite songs to perform.

———————

I grew up listening to Ella Fitzgerald, but I never dreamed that I'd become a dear friend of hers. Ella and I first met when I took my mother to a show for her birthday. I had told my mom that I'd take her to see anyone she wanted, and to my surprise, she requested Ella Fitzgerald. So we went to watch her show at Birdland, in New York, and Ella herself came up to us afterward. She warmly wished my mom a happy birthday, and then said to me, "I love your recording of 'Blue Velvet.'" I was so thrilled that she had complimented me that way, and of course it delighted my mother, too.

Later on, when I moved to Los Angeles, I became close with Ella, who lived only a few streets over. She was an incredible human being; in addition to being such an outstanding musician, she was very humble. When I told her that she was the best singer I'd ever heard, she'd reply, "No, everyone is good! There are so many fantastic singers out there."

When Ella toured with Count Basie's orchestra, she could have flown first class, but instead she stayed with the guys on the bus, to show her support for them. Hers was a version of Duke Ellington's "proper involvement"—having mutual respect for the others you're working with, and not setting yourself above anyone else.

When I lived in Los Angeles, my family always spent Christmas with Ella. On Christmas Eve I would take my daughters to her house, where she would be cooking up the best dishes with one of her friends. We'd go up to the door; she'd open it and greet us with "My daughters are here!" I have such warm memories of those times with her, as do my daughters, Antonia and Johanna.

Ella was a true musician, and her voice was her instrument. Although she sang all over the world, she communicated quite adequately to those who spoke other languages, through her amazing voice alone, and she never needed an interpreter. Her legacy of jazz recordings is a true gift to the world, and it goes without saying that they inspire me in my own work to this day.

———

Louis Armstrong was another musical genius whom I had the privilege to get to know very well. When classical trumpet players first heard him perform, they were dumbstruck: *How did he do that?* No one could figure it out.

Louis was a real original, and he just about invented jazz; he was such a virtuoso. He taught me that being true to yourself and letting your own personality shine through are essential for any performer to successfully communicate with an audience.

If you just be yourself, he would tell me, you will automatically stand out in a crowd—because there is no one else just like you in the entire world. Everyone is an individual; never let anyone put you on a shelf. This was so reaffirming for me to hear, particularly when I was being pressured to record contemporary songs instead of the classics. I knew that I would get nowhere by copying others.

I first met Louis through Bobby Hackett. Bobby and Louis both lived in another part of Queens, and on the occasion when we met, they came over to my house so Bobby could introduce us. In his characteristic growly tones, Louis said to me, "I'm the coffee, but Bobby's the cream." From that point on we became good friends, and we would spend time together whenever we could.

At one point during our long friendship, I was inspired to paint a portrait of Louis. I thought so highly of him, and I worked very hard to make the painting meet my standards. When I finally gave it to him, his incredibly generous reaction put a big smile on my face. "You've out-Rembrandted Rembrandt!" he said. Louis put the portrait in his home office so he could see it whenever he was at his desk. He'd say to visitors who came by, "That was done by a boy who lived in my neighborhood." Louis's house is now a museum, and to this day you can see the painting where it was originally hung.

When I recorded Louis's last hit, "What a Wonderful World," with k.d. lang, she and I wanted to make the song a tribute to him instead of just a cover version. At the end of the song, I added, "Yeah, Louis Armstrong was right. It is a wonderful world." I felt this was a fitting homage to one of the most important musical talents of all time.

———————

Being an entertainer has allowed me the good fortune of becoming close friends with other performers whom I had originally admired only from afar. I had been a fan of Judy Garland long before I met her. She was only a few years older than me, but because she was a child star, I'd watched her in movies since I was a kid. We were introduced in the late fifties when she came backstage to speak to me after my show at the Ambassador Hotel in Los Angeles. I was excited to finally meet this entertainer whom I'd admired for so many years.

Judy had a great off-the-cuff sense of humor, and was incredibly bright and witty. Which is why I was surprised when she told me, once we had become good friends, how badly she'd been treated as a child when she was making films. Even though she was a minor, they gave her pills to stay up and then pills to go to sleep so she could complete a movie in record time. And in addition to the drugs, she had to deal with all kinds of abuse from the executives and producers. She wasn't allowed to grow up normally at all. She always said that Mickey Rooney was one of the few true friends to her in her entire film career. Everyone else had tried to take advantage of her or use her in some way.

"I've never gotten to hold real cash in my hands," Judy also told me. "Someone always pays my accountant a check, and he takes care of the bills. But I never get to see what I've actually earned." So when a promoter asked me, "What do you think Judy would like as a gift?" I suggested he give her a portion of her fee in cash, knowing that she'd enjoy it. He did, and I got a kick out of seeing her in her dressing room after the show. She was throwing the money up in the air, acting like a kid. "Tony, this is the first time in my life that I've actually been allowed to handle my own money!" she said. It made me feel good to see her in such a great mood.

Most people don't realize what a tremendous sense of humor Judy had; she loved practical jokes. I always laugh to myself when I remember the joke she pulled on the great Peggy Lee. Peggy had invited Judy to a birthday party she was hosting one evening. "For this dinner, we're going to have a big crowd," Peggy told Judy. "I've ordered two hundred chicken legs for the meal."

Judy called me to invite me along. When I arrived at her home to pick her up for the party, she had me wait a moment so she could collect her present for Peggy. She got a shoe box, went into the other part of the house, and came back with something wrapped up with a big pink bow. When we got to Peggy's house, she opened the door. "Here's your present," Judy said, presenting Peggy with the package. "Do you mind if I go ahead and open it?" Peggy asked. "It's your birthday; open it up," Judy said. So Peggy opened the box, and sitting there in the middle of the shoe box was a chicken leg—Judy's contribution to the meal. It cracked us all up, and Peggy went around showing everyone at the party what she'd been given.

Although Judy had a really good sense of humor, she also gave me some great career advice. "Of course you need to sing only the best songs," she would say, "but once in a while it's okay to do a number that hits the back of the house; a real show-stopper." She had a good point, and that's why I don't mind occasionally singing something like "Firefly," which always goes over big. She showed me that you can maintain your integrity doing quality work while still including a few songs that leave the audience with big smiles on their faces.

One of the best compliments I ever received was from Judy, who was interviewed by *Billboard* magazine in their tribute issue to me. In the piece, she said that I was "the epitome of what entertainers were put on earth for. Tony was born to take people's troubles away. He loves doing it; he's a giver." Given my respect for Judy and her talent, this was high praise indeed, and I always cherished her statement.

The very last time I saw Judy was in the late sixties when I was doing a televised special with Count Basie in London. After the show, she gave me a big hug and said, "You know what? You're pretty good!" She died just a few weeks later, and I've missed her and her warm spirit ever since. She was such a close friend, one who taught me valuable lessons about how a sense of humor can get you through even the darkest of moments.

For a long time, I had wanted to perform with Count Bill Basie, whom I considered one of the most incredible bandleaders I'd ever heard. It was one of my dreams to record with him. But first we had to deal with Roulette, Basie's label, and with the notorious record executive Morris Levy.

Basie had borrowed some money from Levy, and rather than recouping the advance out of Basie's royalties, Levy simply put Basie on payroll at a fraction of what he should have earned, which was a real injustice. For all of his brilliant work, Basie was just paid a flat fee. Levy said that he would release Basie to allow him to record with me for Columbia as long as we would also do a record for the Roulette label.

I didn't meet Count Basie in person until we started rehearsing. We got along right off the bat; it was as if we'd been good friends for years. At one point Basie told his band, "Anything Tony wants, he gets!"

Making those two albums, which included songs such as "Growing Pains," "Chicago," and "Anything Goes," kickstarted my enduring friendship with Count Basie. We performed together for the next twenty-plus years and spent time with each other whenever we could. I used to bring loads of musician friends home with me, and one night my wife at the time woke up and went into the living room to find Bill Basie and all the members of his orchestra hanging out. Those were wonderful moments, and working with Basie was one of the highlights of my entire life. It reinforced my sense that I had to stick to my artistic guns and insist on doing jazz. If I hadn't, I wouldn't have gotten to know one of the most important people in my life, and those albums never would have come into being. Interestingly enough, that album was ahead of its time, and amazingly, I was the first white performer to sing with the Basie Band.

―――――――――

It is very important for me to really know who my friends are, and whom I can count on. Sometimes in this business, this is an extremely hard task, because everyone seems to want something from you. But I never believed in having an entourage, and I have worked hard to keep myself clear of that pitfall, as it only tends to cloud your judgment. Surrounding myself with those who are tried and true keeps me centered. I value loyalty, and I hold dear the meaning of true friendship.

The Zen of Bennett

―――――――――

When you choose your friends, realize that you are also choosing your teachers.

Proper involvement is friendship that is based on warmth of feeling and mutual respect.

The definition of a true friend is someone who is happy for your success.

No man is an island; you can't go it alone. Friends are there to celebrate the good times with you, and to help you through the dark times.

Good friends bring out the best qualities in one another.

The wisest man relies upon the counsel of his close friends.

Count Basie Band

Fred Astaire

4

Learn What to Leave Out

After years of performing, I've realized that it's not how many notes you're playing that counts, but how you play them. Or, as Louis Armstrong would say, "It's not whatchya do, it's how you do it." It's very important to know what to leave out, accenting what remains—whether you're talking about singing, painting, or just about anything you do. In almost anything, less is truly more.

It's more than just how I sing a song to an audience that gets a good reaction. Many times the order in which I sing the songs makes all the difference. I read the audience and can decide, based on their reaction, whether to skip a song or add another. Or I might have to move a song that's at the beginning of the show to the end. It's amazing how sometimes, by putting a number into another section, you can make a song a showstopper. But in a different place in the set, that same song is just another melody. For me, it's always a matter of trying to arrive at a pacing that's just right for the listener; knowing what to omit so you don't stay out onstage too long.

When I was younger, I would open up with a real hot number like "From This Moment On." I would go out and hit the stage full force, and the band would be wailing. After that number, I thought I would have the audience in the palm of my hand, but when the song was over, I wasn't getting the reaction I felt I should. I remember talking to Basie about it. He looked up at me with those big bright eyes of his and said, "Never open with a closer."

Basie went on to explain that at the beginning of a show, the audience is just walking in, finding their seats, and getting comfortable; they're checking you out. He said that I should stay there right with them and open with something mellow. For the next song I could pick it up a bit, and by the third, I should do a ballad. Then it would be time to hit them with swinging tunes. He told me to save that highly energetic tune for last. And, boy, was he right. The next night I did as he suggested, and the audience went crazy.

So in addition to learning not to overstay my welcome, I also learned about pacing. No one knew better than Bill how to do it right. He had a pure instinct as to what to leave out, and what worked on an emotional level.

Basie just got it. He understood pacing, balance, and how to give the audience what they wanted. Basie told me to focus on the singing and not to talk too much, but to make sure I put a little humor in the set—that it will get them every time. And with his advice always at the front of my mind, I continue to try to do the unexpected, so my set never gets old or boring. By the time the night is over, I want my audience to feel satisfied—and when they feel that way, I feel good.

———————

It took me a while to learn how to edit myself. It's one of the toughest chores to get right. In the first year of my recording career, I released eight singles, but none of them broke through on a national level. By spring of the following year, I was told that I would be dropped from Columbia if I didn't have a hit soon. Percy Faith was my arranger-conductor, and I went to see him in his office to discuss what to do.

"The time has come, Tony," Percy said to me. "You really have to deliver now. And we just have three songs; we need one more." I poked through some music on his desk and picked up a sheet. "Why don't I do this?" I said. The song turned out to be "Because of You."

"Because of You" was released at a time when Columbia had totally lost its belief that I would be able to break out. The song didn't get on the radio immediately, but despite that, people started to play it on jukeboxes. A tune didn't normally become popular before it got airplay, but in this case, that's what happened. After listening to it on jukeboxes, people started calling radio stations and requesting it.

The song reached number one on *Billboard*'s charts and

stayed in that position for ten weeks. It remained on the charts for a total of thirty-two weeks in a row. Finally I had my first big hit. The record wound up selling a million copies, and I was put on the cover of *Billboard*, which was a big boost for my career.

In a way, everything is a matter of editing. No one is perfect; you can't bat a thousand. So if you hear something you've done and it's not right, just get rid of it. I remember talking with Fred Astaire after one of my shows at the Hollywood Bowl. Astaire was always a gentleman, and he would never overtly criticize anyone, but in this case he told me a story from which I gleaned valuable advice. He told me that whenever he worked on a new show, he would struggle hard to come up with the best batch of material he could find. Then, when he was happy with it, he would force himself to cut out fifteen minutes. "No matter how much you love what you've put together, doing that will tighten it up so you don't stay on the stage too long," he said. I caught his meaning, and from then on, I became my own worst critic. It made a big difference in my creative life to realize that it's always good to leave people wanting more, as opposed to the other way around.

It's the same way with painting—after all, as I mentioned earlier, John Singer Sargent used only six colors. The Impressionist artists used brushstrokes to suggest; it was up to the viewer to fill in what was missing, just like when you sing in syncopation. You don't have to emphasize every beat; the listener knows it's there. By carefully editing your work, you wind up with the essence of your message.

I'm always sketching, and I edit as I go along. My art teachers taught me not to show anybody work that isn't finished; the artist should choose the best take, and the rest should be tossed. I'm still working on determining when a song or painting is done; it seems I'm never really satisfied. But at a certain point, you have to stop asking yourself, "Have I got it right yet?" There are a lot of questions that can create feelings of insecurity. You can drive yourself crazy and become insecure, questioning whether something is perfect. You have to understand that at times you're going to hit a bull's-eye, and at other times you need to tear up your work and start all over again.

Occasionally I take a trip to the warehouse where I store my paintings and review them with a fine eye. If there's a painting I have any doubts about, I take a razor and rip it up. That way, I make sure that in the future, there is no chance I'll be misrepresented. This takes a lot of discipline, but I take my work very seriously. I don't want to leave behind anything that I'm not happy with. With a painting, I ask myself what's not essential to the overall composition, and then I work to eliminate it. I always think: *What can I take out?* Then I leave in the one or two things that I feel make it interesting.

In the fifties, Liberace ushered in the over-the-top performance. He was a master showman, and he was the first singer of his kind to play Madison Square Garden. He had been in smaller places with his candelabra and mink coat, but then he decided that he needed a larger venue. After he filled the Garden with his lavish stage production, all the suits at the record business wanted to jump on the bandwagon because they knew artists could make a lot of money by playing huge stadiums. Just like that, intimacy with the audience—in theaters where you could be very subtle and do magnificent things—went out the window. Everything became a quest to see who could fill the biggest arena. I feel that we lost a lot in terms of quality when artists started moving in this direction. Just because you're playing to a large crowd, it doesn't make you the best. My audiences have always responded to the sets that were well edited. Less truly is more, and by cutting back to the essentials and leaving in only the most outstanding part of your performance, you'll wind up with your best possible work.

The Zen of Bennett

It's very important to know what to leave out, thereby emphasizing what remains.

Try to do the unexpected, so people are never bored.

No one is perfect; you can't bat a thousand. So if you do something that's not right, just get rid of it.

Keep in mind that the great artist John Singer Sargent used only six colors to create his masterpieces.

By paring back to the essentials and leaving in only the most outstanding elements, you'll wind up with your best possible work.

The South of France

5

———————

The Art of Excellence

Most people know me as a singer; not many realize that I'm a painter as well. I have the same passion for my music and my art. I rarely consider the two mediums as anything other than the same outlet for my artistic expression. I never go anywhere without my paints, and I carry a small sketch pad with me wherever I go.

The more I paint, the more I realize just how beautiful life around me is. I live in New York City, in a place overlooking Central Park, and I love it here because there's nature right outside my window. I get to see the four seasons change every year, which is magnificent.

The city is always vibrant and so alive. Everywhere you turn, there is so much that inspires me. In New York, I never run out of subjects to paint. This is my favorite place to live, over any other city on earth.

When I walk out of my building, I feel inspired by everything that surrounds me. To me, even a taxicab or a traffic light can be beautiful. Like the tones of a song, the colors of the city are constantly changing. I try to capture those changes impressionistically, whether I'm working early in the morning inside the park, or doing a still life in my studio. I run into fellow painters and musicians in every capital of the world, but in New York, they are everywhere, and I'm proud to be part of the city's artistic and musical scene.

Rembrandt wrote that nature is the master; to me, she's the boss. Experiencing nature and the change of seasons makes me happy and gives me a sense of perspective. We are born, we grow, and then we return to the earth; it's the natural cycle of things. Every time I look at a beautiful tree in Central Park, or the sun setting over the Hudson River, I feel a great sense of privilege. I learn everything from nature; I use her inspiration for my artwork, and I never take her glory for granted. There are miracles all around us every day.

It's not surprising, then, that one of my favorite songs is "The World Is Full of Beautiful Things," by Leslie Bricusse, from the film *Dr. Dolittle*. The lyrics speak to me because I feel that I have seen many beautiful things, and I'm trying to replicate on canvas the pleasure I get from the beauty all around me.

I would describe myself as a perpetual student of art. I'm lucky because I travel all over the world when I tour, so I use the opportunity when I'm in various cities to visit the fabulous museums. I study the techniques of the great masters and try to apply them to my own work. In many ways, art is the same game as music—line, form, balance; how to edit it, and how to make it all come together. You don't just go out in the morning and say that you're going to do a painting. It's like fishing; you have to get lucky and hope that you get one.

I paint every single day; I literally have no choice in the matter. It sustains me. When I'm traveling, I have my watercolors with me. If I see something interesting, I try to paint it, or at least sketch it. You have to know how to draw well in order to be able to paint. And the more you sketch, the better you will paint. It relaxes me, too; if I'm stuck in traffic on my way somewhere, I'll start drawing and forget where I am. My paintings and drawings have become my visual journal; a diary of sorts, of my life.

Usually I'm working on three paintings at once, so I don't get burned out on any one piece. If I feel myself reaching that point, I turn to my music. Alternating between the two gives me a little lift, all the time.

When I approach a canvas, I want to know how I can convey what I'm feeling to the person who's looking at it. I really believe that art should be done with emotion—if it's done with feeling, it communicates more than any other medium. I want to get through to the people who look at my paintings. I use my passion to express myself in every piece of art that I create.

I had been interested in art since I was very young, but after my father died, I was frequently left on my own in the afternoons after school while my mother was working. That's when drawing became very important to me. I'd spend hours trying to get a picture exactly right.

One day as a kid I was drawing a Thanksgiving mural on the sidewalk with some chalks my mom had given me. I was so focused on the picture that I didn't see a man come up from behind to watch what I was doing. "You draw very well," he said. "Keep it up; your work shows promise." It turned out he was an art teacher named James MacWhinney, who lived in our building. From that moment on, he taught me everything he knew about watercolors and oil painting. Even now, whenever I start to paint or draw, I can still feel his influence and the joy he instilled in me. He's the person to whom I attribute my lifelong devotion to the arts.

When I was a teenager, a friend suggested that I apply to the High School of Industrial Arts, since I had applied to the High School of Music and Art but didn't get in. At the time, Industrial Arts was a new school with an emphasis on commercial art. I took his advice, and the experience at the school was good for me.

Fifty years later, I met Everett Kinstler, the renowned portrait artist. It turned out we had both attended Industrial Arts at the same time. The evening we met, he told me he'd been given a scholarship to Music and Art. However, on the very first day of class, the teacher had told him, "I want you to paint what you feel." Everett said, "I'm only fourteen; I have no idea how I feel. I want to learn technique before I can even begin to do that." He left the school and switched to Industrial Arts, where he got the education he felt he needed.

Everett helped me see that Industrial Arts, with classes in everything from watercolors to photography to advertising, gave kids the chance to master all sorts of technical skills so they could pursue a wide variety of careers. Whenever I have a creative dilemma, I always think about what I learned there. Sometimes when I'm working on a painting for hours and feel that I'm not making any progress, I go back to the basics they taught.

Everett taught me that by observing how a painting was created, you can better understand why it is good. I keep this in mind when I view art in museums. I get really close and try to note the artist's technique. When I look at Rembrandt's work, I see the way he left things unfinished. Early on in his career, Rembrandt was criticized for leaving out details. He really was the first Impressionist, two hundred years before actual Impressionism—he was that far ahead of his time. And in the last quarter of his life, when he left even more to the imagination, his paintings became better and better.

Rembrandt is one of my strongest artistic influences; I can stare at his paintings for hours on end. His self-portrait that hangs in the Metropolitan Museum of Art in New York City has always been one of my favorites. I've been coming to the

Met ever since I was a child because my school was right down the road, and I still haven't seen everything this museum has to offer. That's how much art is in there.

What's wonderful about Rembrandt's self-portrait is that as you're looking at him, he's also looking back at you. To me, he's saying, "Okay now, you know me; but who are you?" You'll never forget him because his portrait is so completely honest and perfectly true to life; his face is so alive. No one else has ever painted the way he was able to. I have seven books of Rembrandt's sketches, and every one of those sketches has soul.

Achieving excellence in the things you're attempting to create is truly a matter of patience and learning proper technique. By looking at the paintings of the French Impressionist Manet, another of my favorites, I discovered how important it is to paint what you see. Manet was criticized for making some of his religious figures too humanlike, but he went ahead and painted Christ and the angels that way anyway. Manet's example taught me that you have to take note of what the critics say, but then go ahead and follow your own instincts.

I have so many favorite artists, but two others that really set the mark for me are John Singer Sargent and the Spanish painter Joaquín Sorolla. They were both post-Impressionist; they broke things down into values, as opposed to just color. Nature itself is made up of values; every leaf is different, and no one snowflake is the same as the next. Even though a leaf may be green, it is unique unto itself. Sargent and Sorolla painted in that way, replicating a sense of nature.

Of course they learned from the master, Diego Velázquez, the father of modern art. His painting *Las Meninas* showed for the first time the subjects reflected from different perspectives in a mirror. This is how Picasso came up with the Cubist approach. It's so amazing to think how much there is to learn from these great artists. I always say that I learn more by looking back.

———————

I've had the privilege to become friends with and learn from David Hockney. I attended one of his lectures in Toronto, and afterward he invited me to his studio, and we hit it off. I consider David a teacher first, and a painter second. He's a big fan of ancient Chinese art, and whenever I get to hang with him in his art studio in Los Angeles, he always pulls out his Chinese scrolls and walks me through the way they tell stories.

As David carefully unrolls a scroll, he describes the difference in perspective that comes and goes, so the viewer's eye is constantly in motion. As he explains it, this is how our eyes perceive images in real life. We are always scanning different views of what is around us, including those from our peripheral vision. When you look at David's paintings, you can see that he has taken the Cubist approach to a new level, due to his intense study and understanding of those classic works. It serves as another example to me of how important it is to learn from what has been done before.

A funny story happened with David. One day in my office, the fax machine started spitting out about fifty sheets of printed paper. Each page had an image on it, and we soon realized that it was like a big jigsaw puzzle. When we put it together, it was a six-by-six-foot scan of a new painting David had done. On the image in the painting was a coffee table with a folded *Los Angeles Times* newspaper lying on top, on which David painted a portrait of me as the front-page headline. That's just one example of David's creativity, and also his great sense of humor.

Recently David told me that the young people today aren't learning how to draw, because they're doing everything on computers. But drawing is essential; it's like the foundation of a house. I feel strongly that if you can't draw, you can't paint. It's about mastering the basics before you can move forward.

Interestingly enough, people tend to think that it's an expensive proposition to buy art supplies, but quite the contrary. David turned me on to these certain drawing pencils that you can find in any corner stationery store, and on top of that, they're really cheap. They have the perfect lead point and texture to get the job done right. It just goes to show that you can never underestimate the hidden qualities of the things around us.

British art professor John Barnicoat has had an important influence on my work, as well. I met John when I lived in England in the early seventies, and he gave me private lessons in my flat near Grosvenor Square. He was so inspiring to me, and encouraged me in my determination to become a skilled painter.

I never had an ambition to become a famous artist. Instead, I paint because I have a passion for it. It's as simple as that. When the Smithsonian announced that it was going to include one of my pieces in its permanent collection—in the company of artists like John Singer Sargent, Winslow Homer, and James McNeill Whistler—I felt so honored. I paint for myself and to express myself, but it is still a very rewarding feeling to have my work recognized, as the Smithsonian has done.

Cary Grant was another person who always made me feel really good about my pursuit of art. He had seen my painting *South of France* when I showed it to Johnny Carson on *The Tonight Show*, and he wanted to buy it. I told him I'd like to give it to him as a gift, but he insisted on paying for it. Later when I visited his home, I realized why he liked it so much—the painting looked exactly like the view from his window!

Cary never agreed to do television interviews; he was truly a movie star. But the one time he did was when he bought that piece of artwork. I was playing at the Hollywood Bowl and Cary said, "Let's tell the press I bought the painting." I've never seen that many press agents in my life—thirty reporters were there. I felt so proud that he'd used the occasion to tell people about my work.

The more you learn about art, the better you get at it. Painting should seem to be effortless; it's a matter of concentration and study. I feel that I have a good ten years to go before I can consider myself a highly competent painter—not excellent, but competent. If you're really an artist, you always feel that you could fail at any level. But you have to keep plugging away at it and have faith that at some point you can achieve the art of excellence—or at least come as close to it as possible.

The Zen of Bennett

Nature is the master artist.

We can always seek beauty and inspiration in the world around us.

Painting is a difficult process that has to appear effortless.

Have faith that at some point you can achieve the art of excellence—or at least come as close to it as possible.

Rosemary Clooney

6

Fame on the Brain

I have to be honest: sometimes when I look around, I feel as if I'm from another planet. Over my lifetime I've seen so many things change, and the values of today's society can seem so foreign to me. I grew up at a time when Fred Astaire and Ginger Rogers filmed a movie at the famous Rainbow Room atop Rockefeller Center, and you weren't allowed to cross that threshold without donning a tuxedo. Today when people ask me why I always wear a suit and tie, I tell them it's because I want to be different.

My point is, our values have shifted so much that the world is full of hidden pitfalls. The kids are just starting to reach for the stars, and they really don't realize that there isn't always gold at the end of the rainbow. I know that keeping your eyes on the prize is particularly challenging these days, as we are all inundated by a commercial world. Greed is everywhere; Wall Street is all about "I've got mine, the hell with the rest of the world," and in the end this attitude certainly breeds contempt. We put so much value on how much money we are making that it sends the wrong message, especially to younger people.

Early on in my own career, the legendary singer Pearl Bailey was a huge supporter and believer in my talent. Fortunately for me, she took me under her wing and opened up opportunities for me that changed my life. In fact, the owner of a club in Greenwich Village called the Village Inn would let me hang out there and perform whenever he had an opening. One night when I was sitting at the bar, I overheard him say that he wanted to bring in some larger crowds, and that he was trying to get Pearl Bailey to headline there. After I sang a few numbers, he came up to me and said, "I talked to Miss Bailey, and she agreed to perform here on one condition: that you are on the bill with her."

I couldn't believe it; you never know when lightning is going to strike. That turned out to be my big break, and it's why I became a firm believer in meeting opportunity with preparedness. After Pearl and I worked together, we became fast friends. She gave me many "pearls" of wisdom about the business, but most important, she drummed into me a very important lesson about staying humble. "Son, look out for the fame on the brain," she told me. "Success can be great, but it can also destroy you. Watch out for that helium on the brain."

There is so much truth to that statement. I've seen it happen time and time again—even more so today, when fame is held in such high esteem. You have to make sure that you take care of yourself and don't get a swelled head. You're only as good as your next show; the last one is already in the past. But it's hard to realize this when you are riding the tide of early popularity.

There has to be a sense of longevity about your career—not only instant fame, because fame can go just like that in a flash, as fast as it comes. But if you dedicate yourself to your passion and do it with care, you will always have that to fall back on. So I try to show people that by sticking with quality and staying true to their integrity, they'll have a better chance of being around a lot longer.

Pearl also warned me about how much hard work was ahead of me, and the dues I would have to pay before I could call myself a professional. "It will take at least ten years before you really learn how to walk on the stage," she told me. That was the best advice; I think seasoned performers should tell new artists this, so that any early success doesn't create "fame on the brain" and cause problems later on down the line.

When Pearl married my good friend Louis Bellson, the incredible drummer, we became even closer. Eventually she introduced me to Bob Hope, who had come to see her at the Village Inn. He got a big kick out of me because I was the only white kid in the show, and he ended up inviting me to open for him at the Paramount theater.

At that time, I was using the stage name Joe Bari (after the town in Italy of the same name). Bob thought it sounded a bit corny and asked me what my real name was. I told him that it was Anthony Dominick Benedetto, and Bob said that was too long for the marquee. Then he added, "Let's just shorten it to Tony Bennett." Isn't that amazing? Bob Hope ended up giving me my name. You see, one thing can lead to another. You just have to keep yourself out there.

———————

I have experienced so many humbling moments over the years. Not too many people know this, but Rosemary Clooney and I were the original "American idols." I first appeared with Rosie on an early television talent scout show. A group of producers would then vote for the winner. Rosie came in first; rightfully so. She was a beautiful singer and a good friend.

As it happened, a few weeks later we were both chosen to do a summer television slot on a show called *Songs for Sale*, which was a talent contest as well, but for aspiring songwriters. Rosie and I would sing the songs, and a panel of experts judged the tunes. We didn't have time to memorize the lyrics, and professional cue-card holders didn't exist back then, so the producers just used stagehands to hold up the words on cards.

The stagehands were bored out of their minds and only wanted to get back to their poker games, so they'd hold the cards upside down or sideways; anything to mess us up. The songs were already hard to sing, and we were in a panic every show because we had to practically make up our own lyrics on the spot, live. Somehow we managed to struggle through it.

We'd try to sneak out at the end of the show because the losing songwriters would come after us and blame Rosie and me if they lost; they would corner us and harass us for ruining their songs. We got to be experts at coming up with inventive ways to duck out of the studio, going down the basement stairs or out through the fire escapes. All for the sum of a hundred bucks a week! So this was the start of my big television career. It was very discomfiting, but it was good practice at honing my skill in improvisation. It did feel great to have been discovered like that when we were young, and when I think of the hit talent shows we see on television today, it only proves to me that everything old becomes new again.

Even though the world of showbiz can be full of excitement and new experiences, sometimes getting all that attention can have its downside. There were many occasions when the fans could get out of control. There was one particular time in the early fifties when I was badly mobbed by a group of teenage fans whom we called "the Bennettones."

I was appearing at a girls' school graduation ceremony in the Brooklyn Botanic Garden, right when "Because of You" was topping the charts. The students hadn't been told ahead of time that I was going to be there, and as soon as one of the teachers stood up and announced, "All right, don't get too excited, but we have Tony Bennett here to perform for you," the young women went absolutely crazy and started stampeding the stage. I had to make a mad dash, and they ended up chasing me all over the park.

These girls were running after me like they were possessed;

I felt that I was fleeing for my life. I wound up hiding in a little park shelter, but when they finally got hold of me, they ripped my clothes. I was just relieved to get out of there in one piece.

Aside from incidents like that, I was happy with my new-found success. The best thing was that I was finally able to buy a house for my mother. My dream had been to get her to be able to retire from her seamstress job; that was my number-one goal, and anything after that was icing on the cake.

I always tried to remember Pearl Bailey's words of wisdom about not letting praise or success go to my head. Any artist working today—particularly people who enjoy even a small bit of fame—would do well to heed her warning. When Fred Astaire gave me one of the best compliments I have ever received, I thought back to what Pearl said, even though it was difficult to be humble when receiving praise from a legend like Astaire.

Fred mentioned to me once that he liked the song "I Used to Be Color Blind," which he had introduced in a film. "You know," I told him, "I just made a record with Torrie Zito, and we did that song." Fred asked to listen to the recording, and when he was done, he said to me, "You're it." I thought, *All the humbleness has left me now.* But, joking aside, I was blown away by those simple words. Coming from him, they were very powerful. Still, I remembered what Pearl had said and tried to not let his praise go to my head.

I also try to surround myself with other artists who don't have fame on the brain. k.d. lang is one of these artists. Besides the fact that she sings like an angel, what I love about her is her amazing mind. I first met k.d. when I invited her to sing a duet with me for MTV's *Unplugged*. We performed "Moonglow," and we had so much fun that we've been good friends ever since.

Over the years we've toured together and collaborated on an album of our favorite songs, and she participated on both of my duet records. k.d. is so quick and intelligent with her musical choices and with the moves she makes onstage, which always turn out to be right on. Not to mention that she has a God-given gift in her voice; no one sings like she does. And we both are very honest people, which makes for a genuine performance. She's also a painter, and we always compare notes. Recently she gave me three volumes of *The Complete Letters of Vincent Van Gogh*, which was such a thoughtful present.

k.d. and I did concerts together for a month in Australia, and she's a tough act to follow because the audience loves her so much. One night while we were on tour in Melbourne, I was having dinner with her at the home of my watercolor teacher, Robert Wade, and his wife. When the meal was over, k.d. jumped up and said, "Can I help you with the dishes?" They were so impressed with the fact that she offered to help clean up; it's just so unexpected for that to happen. I love that kind of down-to-earth attitude, particularly from someone who's a big star like she is.

I feel that you have to keep yourself grounded and stay in touch with the things around you that are important. I don't understand performers who get too big for their fans. If it weren't for my fans, I wouldn't be where I am today. I never lose sight of that, and that's why I don't like having an entourage and security guards. I think those trappings just invite trouble. I strive to keep things as normal as possible; I love doing things for myself. There are many days when you will find me with my easel quietly painting in Central Park all alone. Most people are very respectful of my privacy, and I appreciate that. I believe that what you give, you will receive.

The Zen of Bennett

Look out for the fame on the brain—if you're not careful, success can destroy you.

It takes ten years to learn how to walk out on the stage.

You're only as good as your next show—the last one is already in the past.

Carmen McRae at the Blue Note, May '90

7

Never Underestimate the Public

Respect plays a big role for me in life. Respect for oneself and for others eliminates hate, and encourages love in those around us. I'm a firm believer in "do unto others." As long as people are not hurting or imposing their beliefs on others, we should live and let live. Serving the community and giving back are what America is all about.

I've been able to apply this concept as a performer, and I see firsthand how it works. I never underestimate the power that we have to effect change. It's popular these days to put down the public as uneducated, and insist they don't know what's best for themselves. In particular, politicians and corporations have an attitude that they are better than everyone else. This is a joke; they forget that without the people, they are nothing. They think they can just hand them something stupid, and they'll all go for it. Sure, sometimes that works, but it's momentary. There will always be fads, yet those are only temporary. Poor material always ends up in the junkyard.

In a way, I consider myself a public servant; I feel I have a responsibility to do my job with quality, and trust that listeners know what they like, and what they don't. If I were to walk out onstage thinking I'm superior to the people in the seats, I would lose them right then and there. They can sense your attitude. You can't fake it; they'll pick up your body language, see right through you, and say, "This guy is trying to pull something over on us, and he isn't going to be any good." But if they see someone who's in shape, walking out with energy, they're gonna say, "Boy, this is going to be a fabulous performance." They know right off the bat; they're sharper than you could ever imagine. Once you respect them, they'll immediately respect you. But if you disrespect them, they'll do the same. There's no such thing as a cold audience—there's only an inferior performance.

I don't look down at the audience; instead, I look up to them. Yet it's funny how the corporations in America think the public is like cattle. João Gilberto is another musician friend who's also very uncompromising as an artist. He sings very quietly, and he uses an unamplified guitar—no big speaker; just a little microphone so you can hear the natural strings. And he whispers when he sings, in the most beautiful way. João did a concert in Japan, and they gave him a seventeen-minute standing ovation, they responded so well to the excellence of his music.

I saw João perform once in Umbria; it was one of the most amazing nights of my life because I was sitting outside in this very warm, sweet Italian night, with perfumed trees all around us. João came out and just whispered into the microphone, singing very naturally. It was so quiet that you could hear the crickets in the trees. At the end of that show, they gave him a ten-minute standing ovation. Nowadays everybody thinks that the louder a concert is, the better. But in reality, the opposite is true. João gets the longest standing ovations of any artist in the world, because he respects his listeners' intellect.

I found this idea to ring true early on, when I was in the Army. After Germany surrendered, I left the front line and joined the 314th Army Air Forces Special Services Band of the European Theater. Glenn Miller's band had been the AAF orchestra until his plane disappeared over the Atlantic in late 1944. Eventually the chief of Special Services put together another band to take its place, and its new home base was to be in occupied Germany. Obviously the citizens of that country weren't very friendly toward our army, so the new orchestra was supposed to break down some of those barriers. In late 1945, they started auditioning for musicians, and at first I was given the job of librarian. My job was making sure all the music was in order for each performance. But when the officer in charge, Lin Arison, heard me sing, he told me to join the band, too.

We did a weekly broadcast over the Armed Forces Network

that went out to American GIs stationed there and to the Germans as well. The show was broadcast live from the Wiesbaden opera house, which had fantastic acoustics and could hold a couple of thousand soldiers. The band, consisting of fifty-five musicians, was extremely versatile; we could do swing, dance music, bebop, or current hits; even light classical numbers. Lin Arison really inspired us to do our best. He was very creative, particularly for someone in the Army.

Lin had always wanted to put together a top-notch pop jazz orchestra, and he was told by the higher-ups that he could do it. He auditioned for first-rate musicians, and some great players, such as my good friend George Masso, came on board. The band was very versatile; it could do swing, such as Benny Goodman or Count Basie, as well as the current popular hits of the day.

We also had a terrific pianist who played a brand-new type of music, called bebop; it was the first time I'd ever heard of Dizzy Gillespie. I was one of several vocalists, and I usually sang a couple of songs, blues or rhythm numbers. There were a few fantastic female singers who added a lot to the show, too. Some of the numbers that I sang in Germany I did later on in my career, such as "Body and Soul," which Amy Winehouse and I recorded as a duet.

Oddly enough, during this period in the Army I enjoyed the most musical freedom I would ever have in my entire life. I could sing whatever I wanted—if I heard a song on the armed services broadcast and liked it, I could go ahead and do it. The whole band felt the same way. We couldn't get enough of it; when we weren't rehearsing, we'd be jamming in the hotel rooms. Lin let us come up with the most interesting ideas, and everything we attempted went over well with the soldiers.

The GIs were the greatest audience in the world; they were open to all kinds of sounds. Some of the music was rather experimental, but they enjoyed every bit of it.

Performing for the GIs showed me that the average person is much more hip than he's given credit for. That was the first time it struck me that an artist should never underestimate the public's taste. These were guys who had been drafted before they could go to college or barely finish high school, yet they were happy to be exposed to cutting-edge stuff. In fact, they ate it up; they liked the avant-garde material as much as they did the standard tunes. This experience taught me that you can stretch people's tastes as long as you do high-quality songs.

The public is so much smarter than the marketers give them credit for. People are not ignorant; sometimes the record producers may insist they are, but actually most of those producers turn out to be the uncreative ones. The decisions they make are often so far below the listeners' mentality that it's not even funny.

Once I received as a gift a seventeen-volume book on the history of art. The first sentence in the first volume said, "When the uncreative tell the creative what to do, it stops becoming art." So if you're a record company and sign up a singer, you should believe in him. Let him do what he's doing. If you don't like it, then get another artist—but don't tell him what to do. And don't look down on the people buying the records, because without them, you're nothing.

I valued Ella Fitzgerald's opinions, and she lived by these concepts. I once asked her how she was able to be so perfect every single time she performed. "I follow what the audience is doing," she told me. "Whatever they do, I just react to it." And that's the right way to be. If you're thinking, *This is a tough audience*, or *They don't know good music when they hear it*, you won't be able to give them your best.

I view the audience as very friendly. They save up for months in order to buy tickets and arrange for a babysitter, so they are looking forward to having a good time, and to support the person they came to see. I believe the performers who are truly great are the ones who actually like their fans.

Look at Louis Armstrong. He used to do "Hello, Dolly!" six times a night for different shows; it was probably his most commercially successful song. And yet if you asked him what his favorite song was, he'd always say, "It's 'Hello, Dolly!'" When

Irving Berlin was asked what his favorite song was, he would always reply, "The one that sold the most records; the one the public liked the most."

I refuse to follow the trends, because I think so highly of my fans. Any artist who thinks, *They're full of junk, so I'll just give them junk*, is making a big mistake. If you think that way, you won't be around too long. They may love you on the way up, but watch out if you hit a period when things aren't going that well; you'll be a goner. This has been proven over and over again in the music industry.

In addition to doing a high-quality set, I always open with a strong first act. Some performers like the opening act to be definitively weaker than their own, so they appear more impressive in contrast; but I never do that. Instead, I've had Duke Ellington, Count Basie, Lena Horne, and the great drummer Buddy Rich ahead of me on the bill. Of course they went over like wildfire, but I've worked hard at being able to follow the top artists. The best way to win over a crowd is to give them brilliant performers, right from the get-go. Every time I opened with a dynamic act, by the time I got onstage, the crowd was wide awake and on the edge of their seats. They were thinking, *What's going to happen now? How could anyone follow that?* Then I came out and did it. If you have a strong program from beginning to curtain-fall, the crowd never feels cheated.

I love working live. If you have a full house saying, "Yeah, we like this guy," you can't improve on that. It goes beyond what any producer or corporate person tries to tell you is right or wrong. The public always has the final word, as far as I'm concerned. In a way, it's the same for politicians; at the end of an election year, even with all the money they spend on campaigning, they still have to go out and shake all those hands. It just goes to show that if you get the people on your side, then you've got it made.

Having a high opinion of my fans has always served me well. You can't go wrong when you recognize their capacity to understand what you're trying express artistically.

The Zen of Bennett

If you think that you are superior to your fans, you will lose their respect immediately.

There's no such thing as a cold audience—there's only an inferior performance.

The consumer is so much smarter than marketing people give them credit for.

When the uncreative tell the creative what to do, it stops becoming art.

Never underestimate the knowledge or understanding of the public.

Frank Sinatra

8

Butterflies Are Good

For those who don't get up in front of an audience night after night, performing can seem like a frightening prospect. I realize that it must seem completely unnatural for most people to put it all out there and expose their emotions in front of a large crowd. A lot of people ask me how I can just get up there and not get nervous.

Well, to be absolutely honest, any of the great performers I've known do get nervous. This is something most people in the audience aren't aware of, but that's what happens—you get what I call the butterflies. That's really the thing that drives you to do your best. It's the hope that everything will turn out as planned—that I'll remember all the words, and that the orchestra blends with me properly.

At first, I was thrown by feeling like this. But I learned early on that there is a big difference between being scared and being worried that you will do your best. I learned how to welcome the butterflies, because really what it means is that you care, and the show is going to be all right. If you're not nervous, you'll be too overconfident, and your energy level onstage will reflect that.

Everyone who's starting out gets the butterflies, but eventually learns that it's a healthy thing. All the artists (except for Elton John) who recorded with me on my latest duet albums told me they were nervous before we began. I told every one of them, from Lady Gaga to Amy Winehouse, that I was nervous as well, and that it's good, because that means it's going to work. k.d. lang said that the pressure to perform as an artist was similar to being an athlete and having to be on your toes, which I thought was a good comparison. I adore singing with k.d. She is such a talent; she has a great outlook on life and a fantastic sense of humor. She always jokes that the only thing that she and I have a hard time figuring out is who's going to lead when we dance together.

Early in my career, I had a bad case of the butterflies. I had been invited to fill in on the summer replacement show for Perry Como's variety hour, although I'd never done that kind of performance before. When I was having a first bit of success, a drummer I knew told me that Frank Sinatra liked my style. I decided that maybe I could ask Sinatra for some advice, since I was anxious about appearing live in front of a television audience with only a bare stage and a minimal band. He was performing at the Paramount in New York at the time. I had never met Frank before, and I decided to try to talk to him. I went over to the theater and was promptly sent back to his dressing room.

Frank looked at me and welcomed me graciously. "Hello, Tony," he said. "Come on in, kid." (He loved to call me "kid.") I told him how nervous I was about doing the Como replacement show. Right off the bat, Frank said that I shouldn't worry about it. "It's when you're *not* nervous that you're in trouble," he told me. "If you don't care what you're doing, why would the audience care? Then when they see how much the show means to you, they'll love you and support you." I thanked him profusely, amazed at his generosity in taking the time to meet with someone just starting out.

I took Sinatra's advice to heart, and it has helped me immensely throughout my career. It's like a Thoroughbred horse: the one that's nervous and jumping around before the race is the one that usually wins.

The thing about a live performance is, if you sing a wrong note on the stage, you can't just say, "Oh, well that didn't work—let's take it again." You don't want to make that kind of mistake in front of a big crowd. Instead, you want to show the audience the full continuity of what you're doing, so they feel connected with you. You don't want to walk out there like it's just another night. But if you treat them with respect, they'll treat you the same way.

Prior to one concert, Ralph Sharon, my pianist at the time, reminded me that all performers get insecure. "You feel as if someone has to push you onstage some nights," he said. But then he told me, "Someday you're going to look back at all of this, and you're going to like those nights and every one of the records you made. You'll realize that the nerves fueled your best performances." And it turns out he was exactly right. I just released a boxed set of all the records I ever made, and I can honestly say that I'm proud of every one that's in it. Each has the best fidelity, and none of them sounds dated. I can't ask for more than that.

I vividly recall the times throughout my career when I had the worst cases of the jitters. One of those was when I was getting ready for my debut at Carnegie Hall. In those days, most performers played clubs like the Copacabana in New York; it was unheard of for an artist such as Judy Garland or Frank Sinatra to play a concert hall. So it was a very big deal when the promoter Sid Bernstein started booking us in prestigious venues like Carnegie Hall.

To a musician, playing Carnegie is like climbing Everest or planting the flag on the moon, so I wanted it to be just right. Before the engagement, I poured my nervous energy into the date. I figured out the songs I wanted to sing, and I honed them until I felt I was ready. Carnegie Hall had never invited a pop soloist to perform there, so I put everything I'd been studying for the past twenty years into that engagement, which was held on June 9, 1962. In spite of a major case of the butterflies, when I got onstage my jitters disappeared, and it all went very well. My family was in the audience and I was thrilled that my mother was there, too; it was one of the highlights of my life. My mom was so happy that I'd made it to Carnegie Hall. In the end, it was, for me, my most memorable performance.

Another performance I'll never forget was "The Night of One Hundred Stars" at Radio City Music Hall. They had gathered one hundred of the top names in showbiz to perform on one stage for one night; everyone from Frank Sinatra to James Cagney and Gregory Peck was there. I was supposed to come on in a carriage pulled by a horse, and I was concerned because I thought the horse might be frightened by the audience and I'd wind up in the orchestra pit with the creature kicking and thrashing on top of me.

Orson Welles was also part of the show, and while I was waiting to go on, he was backstage. He took one look at me and realized that I was very anxious. "I go to every party at Sinatra's, and do you know, he plays nothing but your records," he said calmly to me. Immediately I felt more relaxed. Then the announcer's voice blared: "Ladies and gentlemen, Mr. Tony Bennett." And I just flowed with it. I got into that carriage, and everything went perfectly. No wonder Welles was such a great director; he knew exactly what to do to calm me down.

You have to walk out there acting confident, and belt out those songs like it's the first time you've ever performed them— but at the same time make it feel effortless. And having a bit of nervousness helps you to do that. Even if I've sung a song for the past forty years, I have to put everything into it, every single time I do it. That way, the audience knows I care about what I'm doing—it can't be rote or mechanical. That's why I try to reinvent a song a little differently each time, so that it stays fresh and challenging for the audience, as well as for myself. I've learned that if you accept what is normally regarded as a negative and find a way to learn from the experience, it will always be to your advantage.

Facing one's fears and taking chances can open up doors that you could never have imagined. One thing is for sure: if you don't try, it's a guarantee that it will never happen. My good friend Quincy Jones has been known to say, "You have to be willing to get an F if you want a chance to get an A." And he has a pretty good report card, as far as I can tell. As best you can, always try to turn that frown upside down.

The Zen of Bennett

Everyone gets the jitters when they're first starting out.

If you don't care what you're doing, why should the audience?

If you walk out there like it's just another night, the audience is going to treat you the same way.

You can use "the butterflies that make you famous" to fuel innovation and creativity.

Lady Gaga

9

Bel Canto

I'm often asked how I've been able to continue evolving as a singer while keeping my voice in such great shape at the age of eighty-six. It's like anything else; you've gotta take care of yourself in mind *and* in body. I make it a point to work out at the gym at least three times a week. I also avoid elevators and escalators, and insist on taking the stairs.

You don't need a strenuous regime to stay fit. As long as you make it a daily habit, even a little exercise can be effective. The same holds true for the voice. The vocal cords are a muscle; if you don't use it, you lose it. That's why I run through my scales whenever I can. It doesn't take much time at all, especially when I apply the method I learned when I was starting out.

Pietro D'Andrea, a talented vocal coach—I named my first

son, D'Andrea (Danny), after him—taught me the technique that has kept my voice strong all these years. It's called bel canto, which means "beautiful singing." This method originated in Italy and was popular in opera through most of Europe during the eighteenth century. The style emphasized graceful phrasing, pure, even tones, and a disciplined form of breath control. It never fails to improve my voice.

Bel canto teaches you to love every note that you sing. It's the art of intimate singing; you're singing into someone's ear. Many of the Jewish cantors are incredible vocalists because they were trained in bel canto. This technique has really saved my voice over the years. I do my scales with a tape cassette of exercises from Pietro. He always said, "The first day you don't do your scales, *you* know. The second day, *the musicians* know. The third day, *the audience* knows." I've kept that in mind, and I always return to the basics to keep my voice in shape.

If you're going to sing, you have to sing in tune. You have to be right on target, as if you're an archer aiming for the bull's-eye. It is essential to hit as close to the center as possible. It takes a lot of practice and hard work to make something as simple as a note sound so perfectly effortless.

The old Italian masters like Giotto knew this. Giotto had been asked to submit a drawing to Pope Boniface, who was at the time commissioning some paintings at St. Peter's. With only a brush dipped in red paint, Giotto effortlessly painted a perfect circle with one continuous stroke. When the pope was shown the work and it was explained to him how it was achieved, freehand with no compass, he understood the scope of Giotto's abilities and gave him the commission. Like singing a note in tune, painting a circle might seem simple, especially considering that it took Giotto only moments to achieve—but as Giotto pointed out to the courtiers, to create it, he drew upon a lifetime of learning. It took years of training and a wealth of cumulative knowledge to get to the place where he could execute something that well.

On the topic of Italian artists, did you know that there are over fifty geniuses from that country, including Michelangelo, Galileo, da Vinci, Fermi, and so on? Italians also created the art of sprezzatura, which was the ability of courtiers to be well versed in almost every science—from the physical to the arts, to languages. And Italians invented the violin and the piano, as well as the orchestra; they came up with everyone playing the instruments together.

All the great masters, whether from Italy or elsewhere, spent decades as apprentices before going on to perfect their work. They learned their craft and mastered the basic techniques until they became experts. Picasso studied the early Egyptian painters and the Old Masters; later on he applied their techniques to his modern works.

As with art, it takes a long time and a lot of work before you get comfortable as a performer. I've been doing this for six decades; I've made over seventy albums, so I've put in the time. Many people think what I do is effortless, but it takes years of practice to make it look so easy. Before I head into the studio to record an album, I prepare. The result is a seamless recording finished in a few days. I recorded *Perfectly Frank*, which has twenty-eight songs, in three days. But before I set foot in the studio, I'd been preparing for three months.

When I was asked to record a song for a movie soundtrack, I couldn't travel to the studio in Los Angeles, so we recorded the song through a fiber-optic tie line transmitted from New York. They had booked six hours for the session, but my son Danny told them it wouldn't take nearly that long. "He records a whole album in six hours," he told them. But they didn't believe him.

The day came. I ran the song down, and there was silence on the end of the phone.

"Hello?" I said.

"Oh my God, that was fantastic," the producers replied.

"I was just warming up," I said. I think they were starting to understand what Danny had meant. We recorded the song in one take. "Wow," the producer on the phone said. "It took you fifteen minutes to do that."

"Yeah," Danny said. "Fifteen minutes and fifty years."

I had to learn the hard way that you have to know the basics of the business before you can expect to succeed. But many of today's artists are coming up out of schools—such as Berklee in Boston or Juilliard in New York—that teach these principles. Lady Gaga studied piano and voice at New York University, where she worked with good teachers, and she's a fantastic singer and dancer. Yet even with all her talent, she was wise enough to know that singing alone would just get her performing in small clubs and bars, so she created a whole show with outrageous costumes and sets. Michael Bublé has a savvy attitude about how to emulate others. He's clever about putting a little bit of those influences into his act—a little Dean Martin, a little Sinatra, a little of me. He puts on a great show and makes it all his own.

I'm so pleased to see that many contemporary artists are getting their education nowadays and are so well prepared. Since it takes years to become a consummate performer, they're getting a jump on their craft.

For me, singing provides the ability to dig deep into my own psyche. The human voice is more flexible than any other instrument in existence. It can express various nuances in tone, volume, and inflections that are beyond compare. It gives me the ability to tap right into the innermost feelings deep in my soul and communicate them in ways that are not possible otherwise. It keeps me in touch with my own true nature, which in fact is a reflection of the nature that surrounds us all.

The voice communicates and makes a direct connection to the listener. This is what unites me as a performer to my audience; we are able to share the experience as one. When the audience listens to me, I hope that, even if for only a couple of hours, I give them the ability to forget about all their daily worries and cares. That's really my goal—to make people feel good through the art of singing.

The Zen of Bennett

Bel canto teaches you to love every note that you sing.

To hit it down the line every time like Federer does in tennis, you have to do a lot of practice.

Even the greatest artists of all time learned their craft and mastered the basic techniques until they became experts.

It takes years of practice to be able to make the best work seem effortless.

Danny Bennett Meditating

The Family Circle

My given name is Anthony Dominick Benedetto, and Benedetto in Italian means "the blessed one." I couldn't say it any better than that. I've been blessed on many counts, but most of all, I've been blessed with an amazing family.

My family came from a small town called Podargoni in Reggio-Calabria, Italy. Around the turn of the twentieth century, my grandfather brought his wife and children to America, and they settled in New York. Originally they lived on Mulberry Street in Little Italy. This was typical, as most people who immigrated to America preferred to stay in the same neighborhood with their "own kind," and insisted on maintaining the cultural customs from the country they left behind.

But my grandfather was an intuitive and astute man. He was

smart enough to realize that his new home was a different kind of country, made up of all different nationalities and religions. He had a keen sense of how important it would be to assimilate, rather than create barriers that would shut doors of opportunity that would otherwise be open to all of us. He decided that he didn't want to live in a neighborhood that was only Italian, so he chose to move everyone across the East River to Astoria, in Queens. The area was a hub of diversity. This was where the workers of Manhattan lived: the secretaries, teachers, firemen, policemen, elevator operators. Among those living there were Italians, Greeks, and Jews. They all lived in Astoria, and they still do to this day.

My father's sister and her husband opened a grocery store in Manhattan and lived in rooms above it. My dad went to work for them and also lived above the store. Oddly enough, the location of the store was in the very place where, years later, CBS—which owned Columbia, my record label—would make its headquarters. When my father was twenty-four, he and my mother became engaged through an arranged marriage, which was the custom back then.

My mother's parents had begun a similar business; they sold fruits and vegetables to pushcart owners. Every morning the vendors would arrive at the warehouse with their carts to pick up produce, and then go out and sell the food all around the city. My grandfather worked long hours at the warehouse, while my grandmother was in charge of paying the bills. Any money she saved, she kept under their bed. My mother went to school for a number of years but later had to quit in order to help out her family.

My parents got married, and had my sister, Mary, and my brother, John. They moved upstate for a while to work in my uncle's general store but eventually moved back to the city. My mother's mom had been so good at saving every little bit she could from the produce business that eventually they were able to buy a house in Queens. The other family members wound up in Astoria, too; my parents followed them and opened a grocery store.

But by the time my mother was pregnant with me, my dad's health was starting to fail, and they had to sell the business. When I was one year old, he was unable to do any physical work at all. My parents moved to a narrow railroad flat above a candy store. It didn't even have hot water at first, and the heat from the kitchen stove barely reached the other rooms, but they made the most out of what they had.

Despite his illness, my father was so giving. He was the person who first inspired my love of music. He had a fantastic voice and got tremendous pleasure from singing to anyone who would listen. My aunts and uncles used to tell me that, growing up in Italy, he used to sing on the top of a mountain near my family's little village, and the whole valley would listen to him. In Astoria he'd sit on our front stoop and sing Italian folk songs to my brother and me. He also used to take us to the movies and read us classic works of literature.

My dad taught us very early on to respect people for who

they are, and not to judge them by the color of their skin. He had great compassion for people who were suffering. He was the family psychologist; everyone discussed their problems with him, and he'd give them practical advice and try to help anyone who was down on his luck. My dad also brought people over to our house if they needed somewhere to stay. Everyone knew they could rely on him to help them out if they needed.

My relatives were magnificent; every Sunday, my aunts, uncles, and cousins would come over for the family meal, and at the end of the day, they'd make a circle around my brother, sister, and me. Someone would bring out a guitar or mandolin, and we would entertain the group. We kids couldn't wait until Sunday; we always tried to come up with something different to amuse them. We were such a tight little community, all depending on one another. My relatives would say, "Oh, you sing so nicely," and "Did you see the way Tony drew that picture?"

It gave us such confidence to see how much they enjoyed our little performances. So even in the midst of the worst years economically, we received this amazing warmth and appreciation for our talents. That's when I realized, *Wow, they like the way I perform. This is who I am*. One of the great gifts of my early life was having this loving family who appreciated what I was trying to do.

All this time, my father's health was getting worse. His heart was weak as a result of having rheumatic fever as a child, but they couldn't do anything for him back then. Eventually it was impossible for him to leave the apartment, and that's when my mother took the job as a seamstress doing piecework in the Garment District. My dad stayed home and cared for us as best he could, but his condition continued to deteriorate.

Ultimately my father just didn't make it; he passed away when I was ten. I was devastated—we all were. After that, it became very hard to make ends meet. My uncles thought that it would be a good idea to send me to upstate New York, a small town called Pyrites, to live with relatives while my mom mourned and got her bearings—so off I went. I hated being away from my family. I missed my dad, and it was an absolute low point in my life. I felt alone and forgotten; I was just counting the days until I could return. When I finally got back to Astoria the following year, I was still incredibly sad without my father around, but at least I was happy to be reunited with my mother, brother, and sister.

———————

Even though our family hit tough times, we focused on what mattered, and we made the best of it all. I remember one Thanksgiving, in the middle of the Depression, when my mom was trying to fix a holiday dinner but there wasn't enough money for a turkey. My mother was crying, and it ripped my heart out to see that she was so sad. I knew that a movie theater down the street was raffling off turkeys, so I asked her to give me a dime to try to win one. I ran down the street and bought my ticket, then took my seat in the theater, but I couldn't focus on the film. I just sat clutching my ticket stub—number four.

The movie ended, and the tickets were spun around in a huge tumbler. I repeated to myself, "I'm gonna win, I'm gonna win, I'm gonna win."

All of a sudden, the man called out, "Number four!" I won! Stunned, I went up and got my turkey, then carried it down the street to my house. When my mother opened the door, they all just stared at me. I've always been kind of lucky that way. For the rest of his life, my brother told this story with the same sense of amazement at my good fortune.

My brother was a fantastic singer; at age fourteen he performed solo spots in the Metropolitan Opera. My mom could afford formal training for only him, and I was always envious of the fact that he got to have lessons. So I felt I had to use my own ingenuity to keep pace and become an entertainer. I'd crack jokes and make my family members laugh, and I loved being able to get that kind of reaction from them. "Someday I'll be a successful singer," I used to tell my mother, "and I'll buy you a big house." In a way, I went into showbiz to get her away from that sewing machine. I'm so thankful that I was able to accomplish that dream eventually.

I have a deep appreciation for what the family can bring to one's peace of mind if there is proper involvement. Today I'm enriched with the most beautiful children and grandchildren anyone could hope for; I'm surrounded by a group of very thoughtful people. They're all individuals, they're all wholesome, they're not stunted by anger, and each one of them means well for the world. Each is accomplishing a lot in his or her own field, and several of them work with me.

My son Danny has now been my manager for well over thirty years, and my son Dae engineered and produced all of my records for almost as long. My daughter Antonia is a beautiful and very talented singer. I'm fortunate that she opens my show now on most dates. This is particularly nice because I get to travel all around the world with her. My daughter Johanna is a very conscientious and philanthropic-minded woman who dedicates herself to many worthwhile causes to help other people. I have six beautiful grandchildren, all interested in or working in the arts. In fact, when we were taping "Don't Get Around Much Anymore," Michael Bublé jokingly commented, "All your family are artists and musicians. Mine are all fishermen. What the hell happened to my family?"

My children have a natural affinity for music. Johanna and Antonia grew up with Sammy Cahn, Frank Sinatra, and Dean Martin. When they were only nine and ten, they sang with Count Basie's band. Danny and Dae attended fantastic jam sessions; Dan once shared a piano bench with Duke Ellington. Dae had his first drum lesson with Basie's legendary drummer, Sonny Payne, who was the first person to hand him a pair of drumsticks. They also got to observe the business of the industry, and watched managers and agents doing their thing, good and bad.

There's a funny story about when Danny met a well-known

jazz artist. Dizzy Gillespie was our neighbor, and he came over and rang the doorbell one day. Danny, who was eight years old at the time, answered the door and said, "Yes?"

Dizzy held out his arms. "I'm Dizzy," he said.

Danny said, "Come on in, I'll get some water for you."

Dizzy told this story until the day he died.

———————

By the time they were in their twenties, both boys were knowledgeable about everything from performance to the technology of recording. That was why, when I needed to organize the business side of my career in the late seventies, I called upon them to help. I asked Danny to review my financial situation, which at the time was in a bad state, according to my accountants. Thankfully, after a while he was able to get my expenses and budget in order. At that point I didn't have a plan for him to become my manager. But he was very good at figuring it all out, and it was a relief to hand those details over to him. So it evolved naturally that he started to manage my career. We began to talk endlessly, and to plan what I was going to do next. And we never looked back.

Danny asked me what I wanted to accomplish in my career. "I want to do what I do best," I told him. "I don't want to compromise my integrity." I wanted to perform for the whole family, and to bring my music to as many people as possible. I also wanted to keep alive the work of performers like Duke Ellington and Harold Arlen, and all the great artists I'd known over the years. I knew that if I brought the best songs to the public, it would work, because that kind of music lasts forever.

Danny agreed that if the younger audiences saw me perform, I'd be embraced by them. He wanted me to focus my efforts on youth-oriented outlets, and he proved to be absolutely correct. In the spring of 1981, I played three New York clubs in one week: the Village Vanguard, the Bottom Line, and Marty's. Then I did a big concert at Carnegie Hall. I also exhibited my paintings at Tavern on the Green, which was the subject of a major feature in *New York* magazine and lots of write-ups in other media. The week was very successful, and I was encouraged by the warm reception everywhere I went.

Danny would come up with some very outside-the-box ideas that no one else was doing at the time. *The Simpsons* was just starting to air at that point, and the creators of the show wanted me to do a song. Danny told them that I would, as long as they made me an animated character. So I became the first in a long line of animated special guests. Danny also set up a feature on me in the new alternative music magazine, *Spin,* which focused on college-age kids.

Fourteen years after I left Columbia, he got me back with the label. He made the good point that most of my catalog remained there, and that we would be able to leverage anything new that I released in promoting any of my previous recordings. CDs were just starting to take off in the mid-eighties, and many people were replacing their entire vinyl collections with the new format. I decided to make a record with the best digital equipment available, which became *The Art of Excellence*.

Annie Leibovitz shot the cover, and I got to record a duet with Ray Charles, which was the first time we'd sung together. The CD came out in 1986; there was a big tour, and I did my first concert at Radio City Music Hall. WBCN in Boston became the first rock station to play my new record, because its promotions director, Chachi Loprete, was a big fan. It sold like gangbusters, and Columbia was happy with the results—as I was.

With Danny's management talents and Dae's expertise in the studio, I made more albums. Each one was well received, and each sold more than the last. When Columbia was bought by Sony, it wanted to do a boxed set of my definitive recordings, which became *Forty Years: The Artistry of Tony Bennett*. That, too, did very nicely, but Danny felt we still weren't getting the attention we deserved. He set up a meeting with the Columbia heads and told them that if they couldn't sell more of my albums, then we wanted out. The executive said they wanted me to stay and asked what I wanted to do for my next project. I told them I wanted to do an album of Sinatra's great standards. *Perfectly Frank* went gold, and I won my first Grammy since "I Left My Heart in San Francisco."

About that time, MTV came into the picture. They asked me to film a commercial for their "I Want My MTV" campaign, which garnered a lot of attention. Then Danny pitched them the idea for me to appear on their very popular MTV Video Music Awards show. After that, MTV decided to add my new "Steppin' Out" video to their Buzz Bin, typically used only for the hottest new rock acts.

I was quickly picking up fans in the younger markets. In the early nineties, I was invited to perform at a Christmas festival held by a rock station in Washington, D.C. The audience went crazy when I sang "Old Devil Moon," particularly when I held the word *love* for an extended number of bars.

A couple of years later, MTV invited me to do their very hip music performance series, *Unplugged*. Dan turned me on to k.d. lang at that time, and I invited her to do a duet with me. I also asked Elvis Costello, with whom I'd worked a few years earlier when we were guests on one of Basie's television appearances. The broadcast performance became the second-highest-rated *Unplugged* for MTV. We eventually released an album of the show, and it became a huge seller, going platinum and winning three Grammys, including the coveted Album of the Year. It was a big deal and turned a lot of heads. All of this was strategized by Danny, whom I credit with revitalizing my career.

My son Dae is an amazing sound engineer. I was honored with two Grammy nominations after the first duets album was released, but he was nominated for eight—all jazz. I couldn't believe it! Dae wound up winning six Grammys. This was just two years after he opened Bennett Studios in Englewood,

New Jersey, and I was so proud of his accomplishment. Danny joined me onstage to accept the Grammy for Album of the Year, another milestone and a personal triumph for me.

When all is said and done, I've learned that family helps keep you sane. Over the years, there were many instances where I didn't handle things on the domestic front as well as I could, but it takes time to learn what's best in the long run. I'm now surrounded by my family; we work and play together. My wife, Susan, and I have been together for over twenty-five years now, and she travels everywhere with me. She brings me peace of mind. Susan spearheaded the creation of the Frank Sinatra School of the Arts in my hometown of Astoria, Queens, which had been a lifelong dream of mine. She also heads our non-profit, called Exploring the Arts, which raises money and makes important financial contributions to support and create arts programs in America's public schools. It doesn't get better than this. As a Benedetto, I can truly say that I am "the blessed one."

The Zen of Bennett

It is a blessing to be able to work with family members.

When you work with family, honest communication is key.

The family circle is one that protects and enriches you throughout your whole life.

Jazz

War Is Insanity

In 1941, when I was fifteen, the United States entered World War II—what Studs Terkel called "the Good War." We were just coming out of the Great Depression, my father had recently died, and the world seemed upside down. My mom really had her hands full taking care of my sister, Mary, my brother, John, and me. Toward the end of the war, when I turned eighteen, I was drafted. I had my basic training at Fort Dix in New Jersey. I knew that I was in for it as soon as I got there. As they do, they immediately started trying to tear me down. My drill sergeant was out to get me right off the bat; the seriousness of what was ahead became apparent rather quickly.

When I was first sent overseas, I was assigned as an infantry-man. We landed in France and marched our way to Germany. It was right after the Battle of the Bulge, and we were sent in as relief soldiers for those who had just won that fight. It was a bloody, bloody battle, and I'll never forget the faces and the psychological trauma of the soldiers that I met coming off the front lines. You just knew that they would never be the same. They all looked like they were going mad and heading straight to the insane asylum; they'd never get over what happened to them.

I watch what is happening today, and it deeply saddens me to see the same thing still going on. It's absolutely disrespectful the way the veterans are being treated after they've put their lives on the line. They need to be taken care of in a proper fashion—given new jobs and top-notch medical care, both physical and psychological. Thankfully, the general public has a better understanding of the effect that war has on the mind now. We all knew men who suffered from post-traumatic stress during and after World War II, but it was simply swept under the rug.

My regiment's job was to sweep German towns for any straggling Nazis. It was a very dangerous affair, and nothing in basic training could have prepared us for what we faced. We were all petrified. When I arrived in Germany, the fighting was still raging, and many nights we were awakened by bombs exploding and gunfire all around us. More than once I was nearly killed. The Germans had this one bomb that made a very distinct whistling sound. They dropped a lot of them, but one day I heard that whistle coming right toward me. It was so loud. *Oh my God!* I said to myself. *This is it.* I prayed that it wouldn't hit me. I remember promising God that I would try my best to be a better person and that I'd go to church every Sunday, if only I would be spared.

Well, it landed right in our trench, no more than forty feet off. It could have been all over for me right then and there. That bomb landed so close that I will never forget the explosive noise it made. Afterward, I did keep my promise to try to become a better person.

That night was one of several close calls. I used to do sketches down in the foxhole as a distraction. It helped to keep me centered and kept my mind off the madness. We saw dead soldiers, dead horses, and huge craters left from the explosions. When you first go to the front line and see a dead person, even if he's the enemy, you look at him and just say, "What a tragedy." To me, it seemed inhuman to kill somebody. After that experience, I became a pacifist for the rest of my life. Killing is the lowest form of human behavior; it's so ignorant for people to maim and hurt one another.

The only good thing to come out of my experiences in Germany was that this was where I had my first real taste of performing when I was transferred to the armed services band as a librarian. It was also the very first time I ever made a record, "Saint James Infirmary Blues." The song was recorded on what they called a V-disc, which the army would put together for the troops. It was a very fragile, cheap 78-rpm record that they could easily manufacture and distribute. A friend of mine located an original copy of my recording a couple of years ago and gave it to me as a present; it is now one of my prized possessions. We just released it to the public for the first time last year.

————————————

The soldiers in my group were eighteen to twenty years old. We just wanted to stay alive and make it back in one piece, but many of my friends were not so lucky. The whole time I was there, I was just waiting for the war to be over so I could go home.

Our company crossed the Rhine in trucks, flushing out Germans who were hiding in towns that were already cleared. We had to fight them from house to house, in town after town, one small village after another. Early on, I was pretty naïve. I had a few close calls, like the time I was standing in front of an open window of a home, only to be suddenly tackled to the ground by an older soldier. He dragged me out of the way, and when we got up and dusted ourselves off, he explained to me that I could've gotten killed by walking in front of a window if a sniper was waiting to pick someone off. It didn't take me long to learn the tricks of the trade after that.

I was passing through a town with the remaining few men from my company, on our way to meet up with the rest of the division, when out of nowhere a German tank descended upon us. Herbert Black, a good friend of mine whom we'd nicknamed "Blackie," and who manned the bazooka, was the only guy who had any ammunition left. He got down on one knee and yelled, "You'd better get down, Tony, because I'm gonna let this fly! It's gonna be us or them!" As the tank's turret started turning toward us, he aimed the bazooka right down the barrel of the cannon and fired. It was a direct hit, just in time. He disabled the tank and saved all of our lives. Later he received the Silver Star for his acts of heroism.

During my time in the army, I helped to liberate the Landsberg concentration camp, which was thirty miles from the notorious Dachau. This impacted me deeply, and further shaped me into a pacifist. Words can't express the emotions I felt when I saw the horror of what had happened there—the faces of the people who had suffered; these pitiful human beings who had nowhere to go. Simply put, it was an absolute tragedy.

Every war is insane, no matter what the reason. It is amazing to me that with all the great teachers—including Mahatma Gandhi, Dr. Martin Luther King Jr., and Nelson Mandela— the great masters of literature and art, and all the contributions that have been made on the planet, we still haven't come up with a more humane approach to working out conflicts. War is archaic. Simply put, violence begets violence; history has proved this to be true. I just hope that someday the people in power will realize that war is not a solution to the world's problems. We only live to one hundred years at most; why use that time to harm others? We should just count our blessings and be happy that we're alive.

The Zen of Bennett

Killing is the lowest form of human behavior.

Every war is insane, no matter what it's about.

It is wrong for people to fight and kill one another.

War is not a solution to the world's problems.

John Heard

Louis by Bennett

Free Form

As an artist, I think that people misinterpret the notion of free form and improvisation. It's often thought that improvisation means that anything goes, but it is quite the opposite. There is mastery to the art of self-expression—knowing just what to put in and what to leave out. It's imperative to master your craft; then and only then can you intelligently make changes.

Louis Bellson, Pearl Bailey's husband, was an amazing drummer who once told me: "You have to first learn form before you can be free to experiment. You can't successfully break the rules until you learn the rules you're breaking." This was fantastic advice, and it came from someone who was known for his innovative improvising. Look at Picasso; his early paintings are classical in style. If you don't know how to do the classic forms of your art, you won't know what to do next.

By studying the great musical improvisers over the years, I've learned ways to keep the public's interest. I try to give them the unexpected so they never know what's going to happen next. They're on the edge of their seats for the whole performance. I always admired Count Basie's music; he was a master of dynamics—first soft, and then loud. There would be unexpected little hits and then a series of knockout punches, *boom boom bam!* Basie's sound was based on the blues, but at the same time it was very modern. His philosophy was one of blending a great beat with a compelling melody.

I never heard Basie play a wrong tempo. He could change up a song in ways I would have never imagined possible. But no matter what he did, it was always in perfect time. This requires incredible care and skill. Only when you have the fundamentals of a piece just right can you experiment with it, as Basie did so successfully. Every piece has a certain beat, and if you find it intuitively, it couldn't be better. Basie was a master of knowing how to do that. When you listen to him, you think, *Yes, that's exactly the right tempo.*

You can't talk about tempo without mentioning Louis Armstrong. He was an amazing jazz performer, and his incredible skill allowed him to be such an inventive musician. He invented swing, a strictly American form of music that will never go out of style, because it's our national tempo. Louis invented bop; he invented rap. Whatever the next category that comes out, you'll discover that he was the first one who did it. Even in the years of severe bigotry, he was able to cut through all the racism by virtue of his sheer genius. He was also generous in his praise of other artists. Once they asked Louis, "Who's the greatest jazz singer you ever heard?" He said, "After Ella?" I thought that was just beautiful.

When I was starting out, I was criticized for making music my own. Musicians would tell me that I needed to sing extended phrases that people could dance to. But as a student of the bel canto technique, when I sang songs like "Boulevard of Broken Dreams," I sang very dramatically; I sang it my way.

Thankfully the composer Harold Arlen gave me the permission to make music my own. Harold, who was the musical director for Harlem's Cotton Club, explained to me that I should use popular music as a tool to perform and experiment with. He said I should alter a song any way that I wanted, and not to be afraid to make it a waltz or a swing or a ballad; to just change it so it worked for me as an artist and performer. His attitude was very refreshing, because other composers would want me to sing their pieces note for note the way they wrote them, and they'd get bent out of shape if I didn't sing it "correctly." Fred Astaire once told me, "Look at the song through the composer's eyes. Then look at it again with a new idea, but one that's true to what was intended." I think that really expresses how to take a song and make it your own.

Astaire also told me, "All I ever tried to do was knock people out of their seats." And he did—in the same way that Rex Harrison and Julie Andrews did with *My Fair Lady*. When they performed that show on Broadway, every single night they sang like it was opening night. That's how it has to be done—just like it's the first time, every single time. The flatness has to disappear. If you bring that kind of attitude to your work, you'll never go wrong.

———————

I believe that spontaneous improvisation—free form—is the single greatest art form there is, and I'm on a mission to teach this to the younger generation. The duets albums have exposed a whole new audience to the ideas of jazz and improvising. Recording duets with such a variety of artists did present its challenges. It's a real game to adjust to the other person's voice, making it contrast with yours. But the contrast is what makes for a good performance. You have to feel where the accents belong, and it's not always that obvious. So it becomes a bit of a game, a back and forth; it's a very creative process.

When John Mayer and I recorded "One for My Baby," I gave John the direction to imagine that we were just two guys who got jilted by their women and started talking at a bar. We threw in things that these guys would say to each other when they were out drinking. It was so much fun to do it on the spot like that for the album, and John seemed to enjoy it, too. He's a very talented guy.

Lady Gaga really understands free form because she's different every time she goes onstage. She played a man so convincingly on MTV's music awards; it was an Academy Award–worthy performance. Gaga is a great example of someone who honed her craft by learning the rules—doing the difficult work of attending college—before she started to break them. She's so creative that if people in the business allow her to be herself, she could become the next Picasso of music.

———————————

I had the privilege of getting to know and performing with Amy Winehouse on my *Duets II* album. To me, Amy sang the correct way; she was ready to take chances right on the spot. She would try a different phrasing in front of an audience, or on a recording. There are a lot of straight-on singers who sound wonderful, but Amy sang for the moment and in the moment, and to me, that's a more honest approach. If there's anything I love, it's an honest performer. She just had an instinct about applying something different every time we ran through "Body and Soul." She had a deep understanding that when you sing one phrase, you have to complement and contrast it with another. And that's exactly what she accomplished on our recording.

Amy wanted everything to go perfectly the day we taped that beautiful song. She was a bit nervous because she hadn't recorded in a while, and she confided that she was her own worst critic. She told me that even if someone else liked one of her records, if she wasn't happy with it, she didn't care what anyone else thought. And she admitted that she got nervous before going onstage, as all the best artists do.

We spoke about the fact that if you come out every night and sing a song exactly as it's written, the audience knows that you don't really care; but if you sing it a different way each time, it means something special to you, because you're feeling differently that particular evening from the way you did when you recorded it. That's what all the great jazz improvisers in the world know how to do. Improvisation was created by the likes of Louis Armstrong, and it was passed on to performers like Nat King Cole, Frank Sinatra, and Ella Fitzgerald. It's about making a one-of-a-kind performance, not quite like anyone else's, and being daring enough to take that chance and hope it works. It's exciting as a performer to exist that way, because then you perpetually grow.

When I taped "This Is All I Ask" with Josh Groban, we discussed how you have to expect the unexpected. Josh said, "You work on it and pace and slide around in your socks at home, just singing the words and thinking, *Maybe I could sing this note, or that*. Then when you record it, every time is a different experience. A lot of what you prepared, you have to throw out the window and use the energy occurring with each new take." Josh noticed that I like it when my band surprises me, and how it makes it that much more exciting to capture the moment. He also mentioned the importance of not being jaded, or on autopilot. All of those things are components of the free form that Louis Bellson was talking about.

When k.d. lang and I sing together, she compares it to a dance or a mulling of souls. She talks about the synergy between us, and likens the way we improvise and react to each other to a balloon bouncing on air. I took it as a great compliment when she said she felt she was being schooled by me, but in actuality she's a true pro who needs no further schooling from anyone.

It's all about the knowledge you accumulate over the years. Once you have all that stored in your mind, when you complement it with your emotional instincts, you are better able to knock it out of the ballpark. You have to be willing to make some mistakes if you're going to go out on a limb. I'm eighty-six; the amount of mistakes I've made in my lifetime seems insurmountable. But from failure you learn to correct yourself and in the process make sure that you become a better human being.

Everyone criticized me for not following whatever new trend was happening at the time. But I found out that the more you go back, the more you move ahead, because you're learning from the best of what has proved to last over time. Then you can take what you know and the skills you've developed to make any song your own, with the confidence to push the envelope.

The Zen of Bennett

You have to first learn form before you can be free to experiment.

Every piece has a certain beat, and if you find it intuitively, it can't be improved upon.

You can't successfully break the rules until you learn the rules you're breaking.

The goal is to create a one-of-a-kind performance; it should be unlike anyone else's.

The more you go back, the more you move ahead.

K.D. LANG (REHEARSING)

k.d. lang (rehearsing)

Charlie Chaplin

Everything Should Be
Done with Love

I consider "love" to be the most important word in any language. It embodies my whole philosophy. Duke Ellington used to say, "God is love," and I abide by this notion. Everything you do should be done with love. It's the greatest thing we can teach our children—to love people and be able to forgive them if they make a mistake. If you fill yourself with hate, you just shrink. But when you can give up yourself to love, you're ahead of the game. That becomes the premise; not anger, not shrewdness. Pour your heart into your work, your friendships, and your family, and you'll be rewarded a hundredfold.

When I recorded my second duets record, we used the Jim Henson Studios in Los Angeles. It was originally owned by Charlie Chaplin. Chaplin never made a movie without love, and as a result, each of his films is a masterpiece. Based on his success, he could have just dialed it in, but he respected his audience too much to do that; he did things honestly. Most of his old soundstages are still there at the studios, as are the vaults where he stored his films. It was very inspiring to record there. Right outside one of the stages leading up to the entrance, Chaplin had left imprints in wet cement of his famous "Little Tramp" footprints. I couldn't resist taking a stroll across them and imitating that famous swagger. Now I can honestly say that I followed in the footsteps of one of my heroes.

I admired Chaplin's work and the love he showed for it, which is why I was so touched by a gift I received from him in the early seventies. One day a package arrived in the mail for me. I opened it to find a canister that held an original copy of the last ten minutes of *Modern Times*, the film in which the song "Smile" (composed by Chaplin) first appeared. Chaplin had heard my recorded version, and out of appreciation sent me this treasured gift. Imagine that.

Bob Hope told me to make sure to show everybody in the audience that you love them, and that you love to perform for them. Not for the money, not for the fame, but for the love of the work and for the love of the audience. I still think about this today, right before I hit the stage. If you don't love what you're doing, there is something big missing. Loving what you do is about humanity; it's thinking about how your work affects your fellow man, rather than just yourself.

Sidney Poitier is a great example of someone who loved what he did, and who also knew how to love and forgive. He had a very tough life growing up poor in the Bahamas; when he came to the States as a teenager, he could hardly read. He was washing dishes in a little restaurant in Harlem when he saw an ad for an audition. He went, and was crushed when he failed because he couldn't read well.

That experience left him determined to transform himself. He not only taught himself how to read; he memorized all of Shakespeare and became a real intellectual. Instead of staying angry, he became one of the most magnificent actors Hollywood has ever seen. He never made a movie that he didn't believe in. For that reason, all of his films are classics. His work is a great testament to doing everything with honesty and love.

When performing in public, I always make sure to follow the advice given to me by Maurice Chevalier when I was first starting out. "Show that there are other artists onstage besides you, and present them to the audience," he told me. Chevalier never liked it when the headline performer acted as if it were only him or her up there, and the musicians behind him were just in the background. So I developed this attitude of always introducing the songwriters and musicians.

Each is a talent in his own right—true jazz musicians who improvise every time. Night after night, they breathe new life into the songs. To perform with such amazing artists is a privilege.

They inspire me, and I feel lucky to be working with them. During the show, I feature the individual artists through solos. This gives the audience a rest, too—they're not just watching a singer the whole time. Proper credit is important; it's one of the few things we can honestly say we deserve, and it acknowledges the people onstage and behind the scenes who help bring the performance to life. I also want to educate my audience wherever I go, so that the names of those great writers and performers will live on forever. It's just one of the ways I'm able to express my appreciation and love.

When Lady Gaga recorded "The Lady Is a Tramp" with me, I was very impressed when she went to everyone on the crew afterward and thanked them all for believing in her and supporting her. I was so pleased to see her do this, and I wish more artists were that conscientious of the other people supporting their efforts.

It's all about being properly involved. Remember, as Dean Martin sang, you're nobody until someone loves you.

The Zen of Bennett

Everything you do should be done with love.

Pour your heart into your work, your friendships, and your family, and you'll be rewarded a hundredfold.

Give credit to those who work so hard to make your performance or project happen.

When you can give yourself up to love, you're ahead of the game.

Lady Gaga

When They Zig, I Zag

Our country has always celebrated the individual; it is the very essence of what it is to be an American. That's what I grew up believing. Whether it's in the arts, science, or industrial innovations, the United States has paved the way for countries around the world, and has acted as a beacon for individual thought and freedom. As I said, my grandfather moved us to Astoria, Queens, for the uniqueness and diversity of the community, so I was always encouraged to be myself. In fact, we were discouraged from copying people around us.

When I was a young boy, I used to go to the movies and watch Fred Astaire on a Saturday afternoon. I'd walk home dazzled by the way he performed. He was a jazz dancer; he never repeated himself. In every movie, he made it a point to do something unique. On top of that, everything he did was different from anything anybody else had done before him.

Early on, I learned the importance of not copying other people's style. I had a great voice teacher, Mimi Spear, whose office was on Fifty-Second Street. That block looked like some little alley in New Orleans, right in the middle of this huge cosmopolitan area. The awnings lining the street advertised the likes of Art Tatum, Billie Holiday, Stan Getz, Lester Young, George Shearing—all there in those wonderful clubs. "Don't imitate another singer, because then you'll just be one of the chorus," Mimi told me. "Instead, listen to jazz musicians that you like, and find out how they do their phrasing."

So I listened intently to the musicians, and I absorbed as much as I could from them. Fifty-Second Street was a haven for all the greats. You could just roll into those little clubs on any day and witness magic. This was the age of jam sessions; when the acts were done performing at 3 a.m., they'd close the doors and keep playing until noon the next day. As a young man, after listening to hours of Miles Davis and all these other incredible players, I'd walk out with my friends from a pitch-black room into the glaring sunshine. I can't figure out how we functioned on so little sleep, but it was all worth it. I remember listening to Lester Young, "the Prez." His sound was so sweet and so new that I got physically sick from excitement. I absorbed the unique phrasing and breath control of masters like Young and Stan Getz in order to hone my style.

When I started playing with bands, I would try to be individualistic and improvise. They'd be in a dance tempo, and suddenly I'd do something entirely new with the beat. Musicians used to ask me, "What are you doing?" They'd criticize me for not keeping the beat, since it was all about getting people up to dance. "I'm being different. That's the way Art Tatum phrases," I would tell them. So I took Art Tatum, and Stan Getz, who had a beautiful honey sound on his saxophone, and I applied their music to my singing. It was the beginning of my finding my way musically and developing my own style.

Jazz is in the moment; it's Zen-like. It never feels tired, because it's full of vitality. Jazz is the most exciting and creative music there is. It reminds me of a sketch, rather than a premeditated painting. There's nothing greater than a Rembrandt sketch; with just a few lines, he could draw the leaves on a tree, where you can almost feel the wind blowing through them. That's what jazz is all about; it's a spontaneous moment that you're capturing.

Today, though, a lot of this has been sucked out of the music that's made. It seems as if everybody has to sound the same and be the same. The record labels find out what sells, and they force all of their artists to conform to whatever that sound is. Instead of celebrating someone's unique character, we applaud the ability to conform. People feel they have to wear certain labels on their clothes and all look identical. This tendency has been a result of marketing companies' promotions, and unfortunately, it has brought us to a new low.

When I grew up, even though it was the Depression, people

were respected by their fellow Americans for their individual spirit; for just being themselves. Of course the big corporations felt differently, and felt threatened by independent thinking, as they do today. If you made it, you made it because you were different from the next guy. Nowadays, it's all been flattened out.

Back in my day, you knew the difference between Art Tatum or Erroll Garner or Teddy Wilson just by listening to them. If you heard all the instruments together on a song, you could tell who the great trumpet player was. You'd say, "That's not Roy Eldridge; that's Ziggy Elman." But today, even jazz has been cursed by elevator music. So you hear a sax with a trio, and they all sound alike; you can't tell if it's a Ben Webster piece, a Coleman Hawkins, or a Charlie Parker, because the producers have congealed music into something shapeless.

Greed has corrupted the process as well. The music has stopped being art, and for many it's become just a way to make a lot of money. But time has proved this to be the wrong path. Not a day goes by when you don't read in the papers that the music business is in decline. The funny thing is that I'm selling more records now than I ever have, when everyone else is complaining that he can't get a break. So I figure I must be doing something right.

Ever since the fifties, I have sung a certain way; I've strived to be myself, and that has always worked for me. I never went where everybody else went. When we started working together, I told my son Danny, "No matter what we do together, when everybody zigs, I want to zag." That's always been my philoso-

My brother, John,
was a wonderful child opera singer—
and a great dresser!

Courtesy of the author

John and me, all "suited up"
in 1941 in Astoria, Queens.

Courtesy of the author

I gave this little boy food from my Army rations right after this photo
was taken in Wiesbaden, Germany, during World War II.

Courtesy of the author

Singing with the quartet from the 255th Regiment Band.

Courtesy of the author

With my Army buddies, the brothers Freddie and Stan Katz.

Courtesy of the author

Columbia's famed studio dubbed "The Church"—it was one of the best studios ever built. *Don Hunstein © Sony Music Entertainment*

My fans have been great to me throughout the years. *Don Hunstein © Sony Music Entertainment*

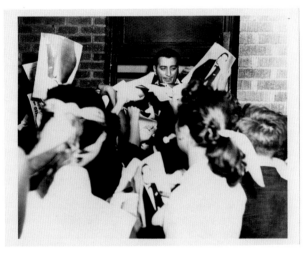

I just love performing in front of a live audience. *Don Hunstein © Sony Music Entertainment*

I had the chance to see Jimmy Durante as a teen at
the Copacabana—it was one of the best spots in town for
live performance. *Don Hunstein © Sony Music Entertainment*

With my mom, all
dressed up in our
Easter Sunday best.
Courtesy of the author

When I record in the studio, I try to get it as close to a "live" performance as possible. *Don Hunstein © Sony Music Entertainment*

Mitch Miller never cared for jazz, but we made a deal that every other album I did would be jazz.

Don Hunstein © Sony Music Entertainment

When I first started out, we would record four songs in
three hours—today they take three weeks to record one song!

Don Hunstein © Sony Music Entertainment

It was a dream come true to record two albums and
perform live with Count Basie—he was a jazz master.

Don Hunstein © Sony Music Entertainment

With my sons, Danny and Daegal—I love the fact that they are so involved in my career. *Courtesy of Sony Music Entertainment*

Louis Armstrong said to me, "You've out-Rembrandted Rembrandt!" He had a marvelous sense of humor. *Michael Ochs Archives/ Getty Images*

Two of my all-time heroes, Cary Grant and Robert F. Kennedy. *Thomas Monaster ©*

It was the greatest honor to march in Selma with Dr. Martin Luther King Jr. and my dear friend Harry Belafonte. *Charles Moore/Black Star*

My mom was loved
by everybody. I still
wear her ring on a
chain around my neck.
Thomas Monaster ©

For Tony—
The Best g.d.
Pop Singer I've
ever heard!
I Love Ya—
Frank Sinatra '86

It was a thrill to get
this signed photo
from Frank in 1986.
Alan Berliner/BEImages

It was an honor to have Valentine's Day 2012 named
Tony Bennett Day in San Francisco. Magic! *VanoPhotoSF*

Piano and voice—I loved working this way with Bill Evans so much.
We made two albums together. *VanoPhotoSF*

Dizzy Gillespie called me up onstage to have a bebop jam session at the Blue Note in New York.
Associated Press

Rosemary Clooney and I were the first American Idols. We started out together at Columbia Records—she was one of the most natural and gifted singers I have ever heard.
Courtesy of Farm Journal Media

I got a chance to see Maurice Chevalier when I was just a kid growing up in Queens—what an absolute inspiration he was for me as a performer.
Courtesy of the author

What a treat to win my first
Emmy Award and have
it presented to me by my dear
friend Carol Burnett.
*© 1996 Academy of Television Arts &
Sciences ©® ATAS/NATAS*

One of my favorite
duet partners—
my daughter Antonia.
*Courtesy of Sony Music
Entertainment*

One of my all-time favorite presidents and people—
William Jefferson Clinton. *Sharon Farmer/Official White House Photograph*

Stevie Wonder played phenomenal jazz piano for me at this session—
he reminded me of the jazz maestro Oscar Peterson.

Mark Seliger

Once, while singing "Lost in the Stars" at the Hollywood Bowl
in L.A., a shooting star went right over the stage. Ray called me the next day
and asked, "Tony, how did you do that?" *Christy Bush*

k.d. lang is so honest when she sings.
I just love her.

Mark Seliger

I have the utmost respect for Stevie—
as a musician and a humanitarian.

Mark Seliger

I love having my daughter Antonia perform on the road with me these days. She's terrific! *Annique Delphine, taken at the iTunes Festival 2010*

My daughters, Johanna and Antonia, celebrating Exploring the Arts at our gala in 2011. Their support is so important to me.
Jemal Countess/Getty Images

phy, and Dan has done an excellent job of making sure that we stick to it. If everyone is going one way, we go the other way.

Toward the end of the sixties, I learned the importance of knowing when it's critical to take bold steps to leave the comfort zone, move on, and take chances. I was going through hard times on the domestic side of my life, and had recently been divorced from my first wife. I was remarried and had moved to Los Angeles, living far away from New York City for the first time, which was a big deal for me.

Eventually, after my battles with Clive Davis at Columbia Records, I decided it was in my best interests to leave and start my own label. After moving to London for a complete change of scene, I created my own label, which I called Improv Records. For the first time in my career, I had complete artistic freedom to record whatever and with whomever I wanted. It was a very ambitious venture for that time; going independent was not in fashion then as it is today. The actual business logistics were quite challenging. In fact, this was the first time I asked my son Danny to help me out on a professional level, which as most people know, led to our working together for over thirty years, with untold success.

Dan was working in bands and following his own talents as a musician, but he always showed an interest in the business side of music as well. He reviewed the label contracts for me and pointed out how distributing records without a major label behind you could be problematic. I asked him to advise my partners of his concerns, but they unfortunately didn't take him seriously. I decided to move forward, as I was excited about the prospects of creating albums that I had long hoped to produce.

One of those dreams was to record with the great jazz pianist Bill Evans, an idea suggested by Annie Ross. With all the albums I've made, the two that I recorded with Bill are considered my most prestigious. In the jazz world, Bill was known as a genius. Nobody in the world has ever played piano like Bill; it was unbelievable. We reached out to his manager and longtime producer, Helen Keane, and struck a deal in which we would record two albums' worth of material. The first, *The Tony Bennett/Bill Evans Album*, would come out on his small jazz label, Fantasy Records. The follow-up album, *Together Again*, would be released on my Improv label.

Unfortunately, his company was quite uncreative in marketing the album; they put it out without doing any promotion, and the sales weren't very strong. But realistically, it's the best thing I ever did. I produced the best music with the best piano player, Bill Evans, and the greatest orchestrator in the world, Robert Farnon—and now those albums live on in *The Complete Collection* box set of all my albums.

I've learned that it often takes five years for something to catch on, and that's what has happened with those records. Sometimes you just have to believe in yourself and exercise a lot of patience. Unfortunately, Improv folded as a result of my business partners' inability to meet the challenges I mentioned, but I remain proud of the music I made during that time, and it continues to endure. Through the experience, Danny had given me some sound advice, which I would later tap into. From the day we started working together, we never looked back, and we've achieved some groundbreaking accomplishments that I'm very proud of. So it just goes to show you that sometimes you have to know what to leave behind in order to move forward.

I try to be inventive when I'm performing or recording. The producers can never figure out what I'm going to end up doing. It's frustrating for them because it's not easy to categorize me; all of a sudden I'll sound different from the last recording, or what they expected or wanted from me. Strangely enough, I've never had trouble with the public on that front; they just enjoy what I do. But I've been misunderstood by a lot of producers and record label people. I never intend to be difficult, but I always have a clear sense of what I'm trying to accomplish. I always strive to be an individual.

———————

Ever since I started performing, I've always wanted to put my best foot forward, and that carries over to the way I dress on-stage. I think it shows respect for the people who've gone to the trouble to come out and see me perform.

I was watching television at 2 a.m. one night when a documentary about Andy Warhol came on. It caught my interest because I had known Andy pretty well. They were asking him about changes in society and the fact that no one wears a suit any longer. The speaker asked him, "Is there any glamour left?" and Andy said, "Yeah." All of a sudden there's a picture of me with Andy at a Hollywood party. "Tony Bennett's the only one keeping it with the glamour," Andy said.

I've been in three earthquakes, and one was in Japan with Count Basie's band. It lasted for an entire minute, and the band ran out into the street in the middle of the night. Funny enough, I slept through the whole thing, and the band kidded me for the rest of the tour because I missed it. I was lucky it wasn't a bad one.

But the earthquake I'm known for was a big one in Los Angeles. The whole chest in the bedroom came down with the television on it and everything; it went *bam!* right next to my bed. It was four o'clock in the morning, and my hotel was evacuated. I went outside, and there was everybody in their pajamas and bathrobes. I was the only one who'd put on a suit. Most people were shocked, and asked me if I slept in my formal wear. When a reporter interviewed me about the incident, he asked why I had a suit on in the middle of the night. I said that it was because I was voted Best Dressed Man that year and had to live up to that image. But, joking aside, if you respect someone and also have strong self-respect, you'll take the trouble to look your best. Putting that extra effort into my appearance translates into showing that I care about what I do—and the audience picks up on that.

Speaking of zigging and zagging, Lady Gaga looked fantastic when she arrived to record "The Lady Is a Tramp" with me.

She came dressed to the nines in a beautiful full-length black lace dress, and her hair was a striking shade of aquamarine. Gaga is someone who is not afraid to be different, and who has built a whole career around that. We realized we have a great affinity with each other on this front. When I told her that I loved the way she looked, she said, "Thank you, Tony. I thought I'd give it a little twist for you. I said, 'What would Tony want?'"

Then she told me I looked handsome, and wanted to know if I chose the yellow shade of my glasses intentionally. When I told that her I did, she gave me a knowing look of approval and said, "I figured." She could tell exactly what I had in mind.

Gaga was also intrigued by my past; she asked me what it was like with the girls when I started out. She wanted to know if they got nervous and started blushing around me like she was; she was imagining what it must have been like when I was a young pup. "I would've been chasing you around in this dress," she said, which made me feel quite flattered. Lady Gaga was a joy to work with; she came to the session totally prepared, and the chemistry between us was all sparks.

Later I painted Gaga's portrait for a photo shoot for *Vanity Fair* with photographer Annie Leibovitz behind the camera. She was a natural model—and I'll tell you, she was as professional and elegant undressed as she was dressed. We had a lot of fun together, and we have since become great friends.

"Vive la différence," I love to say. Hanging out with people who aren't exactly like you keeps life interesting, and also keeps you on your toes. Andy Warhol once told me: If you have an idea, but you don't execute it, then it's just an idea. But if you do it, then it becomes a fact. That statement always stuck with me, and spurred me on to try new things. I'm always seeking to find new meaning in a song, every time I sing it.

I'm very satisfied when one of my songs comes on the radio and people say they can tell right off the bat that it's one of mine. Then I know that I've done what I set out to accomplish. If you strive to be yourself at all times, you'll just naturally be different from the pack. Remember that no two snowflakes are alike!

The Zen of Bennett

Don't imitate another person, because then you'll just be one of the chorus.

If you create good music, no matter what year it came out, it will always sound completely modern.

Use the past to memorize the mistakes you've made, and make sure you don't repeat them.

When you are yourself, you automatically become different from everyone else.

Sinatra

Mentor a Young Person

An old Chinese proverb states, "If you want to learn something, go to someone older than you, because they've lived longer." My grandfather and father were philosophers, so to speak; the entire neighborhood would come to them for advice. Throughout history the elders in any society were always granted that kind of respect. Only recently has society moved in the direction of discounting the elderly. This attitude really makes no sense; older people have lived longer and have more experience; they are entitled to and deserve respect.

At the same time, I feel it's the responsibility of the elders to pass on the lessons they've learned, and not to disdain those younger than they are. George Bernard Shaw was known for saying, "Youth is wasted on the young." To a certain extent, this is true, but it only serves to support the idea that we have a lot to teach those who are just starting out. I believe that a great deal of energy should be dedicated to doing just that.

———————

When Rosemary Clooney and I first started out, the seasoned performers we met didn't pull any punches with us; they told it like it was. They said, "It's going to take six years before you become a consummate performer." That came as a shock to me, but it turned out to be right on the money. And it was a tough pill to swallow, because we weren't really allowed in the club until then.

Many years later, I realized that I was becoming the elder statesman, and I wanted to make sure the up-and-comers didn't have to go through what I did. It's inevitable—they're going to become the masters eventually. I don't want to act as if it's impossible for them to succeed, which was the sentiment that some people expressed to me when I was coming along.

I'm offended by the way younger performers are often treated today. They're led to believe by their agents and lawyers and managers that it's all about the money and the fame. Most of them wind up failing miserably, while the people in the background are the ones cashing in. It should be quite the opposite: it's the artists who give the power to the agents and lawyers and record companies. Without the artists, these handlers would be nothing.

It's more dangerous out there than ever. One minute, a brand-new singer is an American idol; she may rise to the top of the charts and fill the stadiums in a year or so. But as soon as the crowds thin out and the records stop selling, she's finished, and the company goes after the next act. This is just cruel. I believe in the importance of training young, raw talent so they produce work that will last; otherwise they'll burn out fast, and find themselves left with no career to build on.

I want to help these artists learn how to simplify things; to understand the power of standing in a spotlight—just them and the music—and of singing a classic song. I advise them that fame comes and goes, but longevity is the thing to aim for.

I also stress keeping things relaxed. The more relaxed, the more peaceful, the better, and the more successful you will be. Like the Zen masters say, it's like water flowing over a rock. The water is fluid and basic, but over time, it's powerful enough to mold the rock to its shape. It just requires patience, and being able to learn from your mistakes.

I made so many mistakes when I was younger. I had a great desire to be a singer, but I went to many auditions where I didn't get the job. Having the courage and faith to continue helped me hold on to my desire to sing. I realized that I would have to work at it. You start out as an amateur and have to persevere for a number of years before you become a professional.

An "amateur" can be defined as someone who loves what he or she is doing as a pastime. The difference for those who go on to be professionals is that they really have no choice in the matter. They were born to do what their passion is. They are driven beyond the point where failure is an option. I always say I had no choice but to be a singer; it's what I was meant to do. It's like breathing; it's not something you think about.

People often confuse being a successful artist with being commercially successful, but they are not one and the same. I've known many magnificent artists who were at the top of their game but didn't make a red cent from their work. Was Van Gogh "successful"? He sold only one painting in his lifetime, and that was bought for four hundred francs. Van Gogh died broke, but I dare anyone to challenge his genius. It's a pity; I wonder what he would think if he could sit in the back of Christie's auction house today and watch his paintings sell for multimillions of dollars. Sometimes there is no justice, but when you are coming up, it's important to keep in mind the difference between being a successful artist and being commercially successful.

Those "amateurs" who have no choice but to do what they do will become the new masters eventually, so I say, why not help them along? After all, so many people helped me when I was starting out. I've mentioned that Pearl Bailey gave me my start at the Village Inn by insisting that I open for her. Bob Hope was another artist who helped me quite a bit. The first time I ever saw Bob in person was when I attended his show as a GI in Germany. It was absolutely the best thing that had happened to me over there. The show was wonderful, and it made me realize that the greatest gift you can give is to lift someone's spirits with a joke or a song.

After Pearl Bailey brought Bob to catch my act at the Village

Inn, he invited me to sing at the Paramount with him, which was another huge break for me. When I finished singing, Bob said to the audience, "Well, I was getting tired of Bing anyway!" Then, when the Paramount engagement was over, Bob took me on a six-city tour along with the rest of the troupe. He also introduced me to Bing Crosby when Bing stopped by the show, which was such a thrill. I didn't really know how to act while I was singing, but Bob showed me that it's important to be upbeat when you walk out on the stage. The audience needs to know that you're happy to be there and that you can't wait to entertain them; all these years later, I'm still using that advice.

It was Benny Goodman who taught me how to work a microphone. "Don't eat it," he said. "Just step away from it and be natural." He taught me to hold the mic, not attack it. That way the audience can better hear how I sing. That technique also helps to hold the listeners' attention because it's not quite as loud.

My greatest mentor was Frank Sinatra. To me, he made the best music that ever came out of this country. He had a magical voice, and he was able to communicate exactly what he was feeling. He knocked down the wall between himself and his audience, and let people inside his head. Before he came along, no one had ever sung so personally or vividly.

In 1960, Sinatra did a wonderful thing for me. I was working with Duke Ellington at the Americana Hotel in Miami Beach, and he and Joe E. Lewis rounded up every hotel owner they knew and brought them to see me perform. From that show alone, for the next two decades, I got booked into places such as the Waldorf-Astoria in New York, the Hilton in Las Vegas, and the Palmer House in Chicago. It was a great boost for my career.

Sinatra was always supportive of me, but in April 1965 he did the unimaginable: he announced in *Life* magazine that I was his favorite singer. "For my money, Tony Bennett is the best singer in the business." Sinatra told the interviewer, "He excites me when I watch him. He moves me. He's the singer who gets across what the composer has in mind, and probably a little more."

This statement blew me away, and literally changed my life. After Frank said I was his favorite, everyone wanted to hear me perform. It was probably the single most generous thing any artist had ever done for another.

When Frank broke his arm and couldn't perform at a benefit for an Italian-American senior citizens' home in Chicago, I agreed to do it instead. At the last minute Frank realized that he could do the show after all, so we decided to perform it together. Frank wanted to go on first, and after he finished, he said, "Ladies and gentlemen, the greatest singer in the business—Tony Bennett." That was an honor I'll never forget.

Frank and I never lived in the same place except when I was in Los Angeles in the early seventies, and we didn't get to spend a lot of time together because we were both on the road so much. But it was always special to be in his presence, especially when we were performing together. In 1977, he invited me to sing on his ABC TV special, *Sinatra and Friends*. I did "One" from *A Chorus Line*, then Frank and I sang "My Kind of Town" as a duet. It was a thrill to be able to do the show with him, particularly since he had given me such great advice over the years about performing.

I always picked up lessons from people who'd been in the business before me, and now I like to pass along the friendship and generosity to a younger generation. I enjoy the fact that by doing the duets, I can showcase another artist and welcome them into the club. I encourage them to ask me about the trials and tribulations, the ups and downs, what to look out for when they get into trouble, or when to accentuate something that's good. It feels great to be able to support this amazingly talented new generation of performers.

The Zen of Bennett

Fame comes and goes, but longevity is the thing to aim for.

By doing quality work, you'll always be around.

You have to work at your art. You start out as an amateur, and need to persevere for a number of years before you become a professional.

If you want to learn something, go to people who are older than you, because they've experienced more and can pass on what they've learned.

Triborough Bridge From Astoria, June '86

Black Crows and Golden Birds

The hardest part about being a performer is that you are always under scrutiny. I try not to read my own reviews, because when someone writes about you, it's not easy to be objective. I relish constructive criticism, but mostly from people I trust who have no other agenda than my best interests at heart.

History has shown how wrong critics can be; dating back to the earliest printed word, there are endless examples of write-ups that were so far off-base that it's almost an honor to join the long list of successful artists who were told they'd never amount to anything. It takes a lot of self-confidence to forge ahead when someone out there deems your work unworthy, but for me, overcoming adversity has always come with the territory. In the end, it really builds character. What may appear as a negative event can have a positive outcome if you only learn to apply yourself in a proper fashion. I always try to keep an open mind, but it's important to be determined to get things done in the way you envision them. Most of the time you just have to get it right for yourself.

Throughout my life, I've run into much criticism and many obstacles that could have made me give up following my dreams. There was a lot of pressure from some of my family members; when I first started performing, they even called me a gigolo. They said, "Why don't you get a regular job and help your mother; she is working so hard." But I always wanted to work at something I loved. I realized that I had to follow my passion and bliss, and take what others said with a grain of salt, in order to live my dream and do what I was good at.

Even as a kid, I ran up against people who discouraged my desire to perform. When I was in grammar school, I had one teacher who separated the class into "golden birds"—the children she felt could sing in tune—and "black crows"—those she thought couldn't sing worth anything. After she heard me, she said, "You're definitely a black crow."

At first I was taken aback by that comment, but once I got over my initial discouragement, I decided to try to prove her wrong. After all, my family seemed to love it when I sang at home, so I figured I must have some talent in that area. Eventually that "crow" comment helped shape my attitude about persevering and believing in myself, despite the naysayers. And in the years to come, I ran into many of them. In fact, just before he died at the age of ninety-nine, Mitch Miller called up Danny and admitted that even though all those years ago he told me being a jazz singer would destroy my career, history has shown that it sustained my career instead, and that I was bigger than ever. Mitch concluded, "Boy, was I wrong on that one!"

After the teacher who made the "black crow" comment, I was lucky enough to have a teacher who was very nice. She gave me the role of the prince in our first-grade production of *Snow White*, and she treated me very kindly. Then when I was nine, another teacher, Mrs. McQuade, arranged for me to sing at the local Democratic club, and also alongside New York mayor Fiorello La Guardia at the grand opening of the Triborough Bridge in 1936. Three years earlier, then-candidate La Guardia had promised that if he got elected, he would finish construction, which had been sputtering along in fits and starts for a number of years. So it was a big deal when it finally was completed. There was a huge celebration, and Mrs. McQuade had me standing right next to the mayor when he cut the ribbon. After the speeches, I got to lead the group across the new bridge, singing "Marching Along Together." Mrs. McQuade believed in me, and that early public performance confirmed my desire to be an entertainer.

When I was sixteen, I ran into a stumbling block when I had to drop out of the School of Industrial Arts to help my mom. She was working her fingers to the bone trying to make ends meet, and I needed to contribute to the family's income. I worked as an elevator operator, but I couldn't get the darn thing to stop in the right spot! People had to crawl out between the floors. That didn't go over too well with the tenants, and it quickly put an end to that job.

Next I found work at a laundry, and after that I took a position as a copyboy for the Associated Press, running around with papers. I got fired from that one, too. It soon became apparent to me that I couldn't hold down any of these jobs to save my life. It brought into focus the fact that if my heart was not in what I was doing, I would experience nothing but failure.

I found my true calling only when I began performing at amateur nights in Brooklyn, Queens, and the Bronx. People would get up onstage and perform in front of an audience, which would then vote on the performer they liked the most. The favorite got a small percentage of the door, and I was lucky enough to win a number of times. My biggest competition was from this guy who came on in a sailor's uniform with a fake cast on his leg; he knew how to manipulate the audience to think he had been serving in the war. When he sang "My Mother's Eyes," he'd have everyone in tears. Whenever he showed up, I'd think, *Great, there go my winnings for the week.* I'd like to see anyone else try to follow that act!

It was at that time that I started working as a singing waiter at a restaurant in Astoria. A customer would request a song, and I'd run into the kitchen to work out the arrangement. There were a couple of great Irish waiters who taught me all the best standards. You know, it's a funny thing; now whenever I go to Italy, I notice that all the waiters are great vocalists—they perform at the drop of a hat. They actually give me a complex, they're so good.

Cutting my teeth as a singing waiter was the most valuable experience I ever had as a performer; it was a real trial by fire. I was literally singing for my supper. It was the best way for me to learn to follow my artistic instincts as I worked for the first time in front of a live audience that I had to win over. The experience was not unlike when I ended up singing in the armed services band a couple of years later.

It was during my stint overseas with the Special Services Band that I really caught the bug for entertaining. When I returned home, I was determined more than ever to do what I needed in order to be a performer—even if that meant knocking on the doors of every club and promoter in New York City. I went to audition after audition, but I got turned down every time. This was kind of surprising to me, since I'd received such good feedback when I was with the band in Germany. But the rejections didn't stop me; I just kept at it. I even tried out for a chorus part in a Broadway show, but I didn't get that, either.

I took every opportunity to sing in any club or restaurant—unpaid, of course—just to have the experience, and to work with some terrifically talented jazz musicians. I did many things the wrong way, but that was how I learned. Only by sticking with it would I accomplish what I wanted. Everyone is faced with challenges; I realized that I simply couldn't lose heart.

It was tough getting started—it took about seven years to

really get going. When I listen to early recordings of myself before I was signed to Columbia, I can't believe how much I had yet to learn back then. But certain people were wonderfully supportive and encouraging. One was Barbara Carroll, the jazz pianist and vocalist. She'd always say, "Come on, get up and sing with me. Maybe somebody important will come in and listen to you, and give you a break." For years she helped me out; she's such a magnificent person, and a big talent in her own right.

Around this time I was hanging out with a friend from Queens, Jack Wilson, who also wanted to make it in the music business. Jack was a songwriter, and we scraped our money together to buy the latest records and memorize all the tunes. We'd sing on the street corners sometimes, and we'd go into midtown Manhattan and catch the big band shows. I also met Abby Mann, a struggling young screenwriter and director, and the three of us talked about doing a musical comedy. (Abby later won the Oscar for his great screenplay of *Judgment at Nuremberg.*)

Another friend from this time was Freddy Katz, whose parents were like family to me and hosted jam sessions in their home on Friday nights. I introduced Jack to Freddy, and we combined our efforts: Jack wrote the words, Freddy wrote the music, and then the three of us visited record companies in the city to perform our compositions in the hopes of getting a contract. Freddy was so talented that eventually he wound up playing with Lena Horne and Vic Damone.

I finally got a gig in a nightclub that was located right under the el train in Astoria. I had sung informally at the bar, and the band's trombonist, Tyree Glenn, let me sing with them for a while until he joined Duke Ellington's orchestra. Then I took another job as a singing waiter, and I got to perform at some bars and clubs in Manhattan. A tiny place in Queens, the Nestle Inn, let me sing with Stan Weiss's group, which was playing there. During this period I'd go with my friends to hear great jazz on Fifty-Second Street, where all the best clubs were, and just dream about the day when I could be a professional performer. I never did get a paying gig on Fifty-Second Street, although I practically lived there for several years and sang for free in a few places, just to try to get some exposure.

All this time, I was living on one dime per day. My mother gave me some change before she left for work, but I never took more than ten cents. I'd go to the city and make my rounds, using the money to buy a bite to eat. Some family members, such as my mother's relatives, complained about my pursuing a career as an entertainer; they thought I should buckle down and do something more useful. But I was determined to make it as a performer, even if I wound up being a singing waiter for the rest of my life. In fact, that's exactly what I would have done if I hadn't ever gotten a recording contract.

Eventually through Freddy Katz I found my first manager, Ray Muscarella, and finally I felt as if someone could get me some legitimate bookings. Ray thought my singing was a little rough around the edges, so he hired a coach to help me hone my act. After a while he got me a paying gig at a club called the Shangri-La in Queens, and then a spot on the *Arthur Godfrey's Talent Scouts* program—the one I appeared on with Rosemary Clooney, and the model for shows like *American Idol*. As I mentioned before, Rosie and I wound up working together on a summer television show.

A while later, we both were signed to Columbia Records. Even though Rosie and I each ended up having a couple of million-selling albums, when we'd run into the masters, like Jack Benny or George Burns or Bob Hope, they'd say, "You're doing great, but it's going to take time before you really know how to handle an audience." They told us not to rest on our laurels, and that we were just going to have to learn the hard way. They all had come from vaudeville; that's where they cut their teeth. They would play in theaters all over the United States and the world on a nightly basis, where the people in the seats became the teachers. The audience let the performers know right then and there what they liked and what they didn't like, if they were onstage too long, and how to give the audience just enough. I would learn from the audience, too, but it would take time. Sure enough, about six years later, Bob Hope came to see me at the Fairmont in Dallas. When the show was over, Hope confirmed, "You've finally become a consummate performer."

My song "Boulevard of Broken Dreams," from my first recording for Columbia Records, was a big hit, and I thought I had it
made. I felt elated by my success, so I took two weeks off and
went on vacation in Puerto Rico. After I returned, I released
eight singles, one after the other, but none of them took off.

Columbia was about to let me go, and I was desperate.
Thankfully, my next single, "Because of You," went to number
one on the charts. I relaxed quite a bit and the record label was
happy for a while, but I had learned an invaluable lesson: never
take anything for granted. I still had to earn my stripes every
day. Almost being dropped from the label spooked me so much
that I didn't take another vacation until I was well into my seventies. That's the honest truth! Finally I'm confident enough
to travel every year to Italy with my wife, Susan, for at least a
month. I relax, paint, and enjoy the food and the people. Better
late than never, I guess.

But back then, I was still paying my dues. I started having a
string of number-one hits, and I was playing clubs all day and
all night; places like the Paramount and the Copacabana. At
the Copa, you did three shows a night. We'd start at eight p.m.,
and we wouldn't get out of there until four in the morning. If
there was a blizzard, we'd go out the back entrance and have
to wade through huge drifts of snow. Then at the Paramount,
which was considered the big time, we'd do seven shows a day,
ten thirty in the morning until ten thirty at night. That really

separated the men from the boys. Nowadays it's usually one show a night, which is a much better pace. But that kind of grueling schedule, as inhuman as it seemed, forces you to hone your performance.

By the mid-fifties, I was recording two or three albums a year, a pace I kept up for the next two decades. On top of this I was performing around two hundred dates a year. I'd come home, make a record, and leave; it wasn't great for my family life. But there weren't as many artists back then, so in order to meet the demand, you had to put out new material constantly. There were a lot of deadlines to meet, and it was a shock to me how challenging it was to make each record better than the last one. We singers aren't machines; you can't just crank it out every single time. Some records are right in there, and others you feel could have been a little better.

That said, unconstructive criticism can have a strong effect on even the best performers. It seems that many people who fail at what they try to do wind up critiquing. Recently I read a book about Fred Astaire that said that early on in his career, he was extremely upset by the harsh words of a bad review. It made such a deep impression on him that it haunted him for years. And that man was a genius!

I had a similar experience when I did my first concert at Carnegie Hall. I had prepared for that show like nothing ever before, and the audience loved the concert. But a critic from a major newspaper lambasted the performance, and it affected me for quite a while afterward. Yet fifty years later, the show is now widely acclaimed as one of the best concerts ever recorded. That just goes to prove that you have to believe in yourself.

Another test in perseverance came during the period from 1977 to 1986, after I recorded the second Bill Evans album. Although I continued to do concerts, this was a quieter time for me, and I didn't put out any new material. My career began to take off again in the early eighties, but even so, it took a few years before my son and manager Danny set up recording *The Art of Excellence* and we truly hit our stride again. It felt great to be back in the studio, and more than anything, the experience showed me that if you stick to your guns about doing quality work, you will always have an audience.

———————

Despite being told by my teacher that I had the voice of a crow, I ended up performing for every U.S. president since Eisenhower. I've come a long way. (Of all the presidents I've performed for, Bill Clinton has put me at the greatest ease. I don't have to stand at attention, or feel that I'm talking to an emperor; he always acts like a human being. And by the way, Clinton is also fantastic at harmonizing. Once at a fund-raiser, I saw him waiting to go onstage while a band was playing, and he was humming right along in perfect key. He is a real musician.)

With all of my command performances, Grammys, and

other awards, many people assume that I've been on top for my entire career. However, everyone has dips and curves, peaks and troughs. Still, I'm living proof that if you stick to doing what you love, and believe in yourself, you will come through victorious in the end.

The Zen of Bennett

Be determined to persevere, even in the face of criticism.

Realize that everyone has setbacks, particularly when starting out.

Don't let the naysayers get you down.

Obstacles are necessary for success. Be persistent and you will reach your goals.

San Francisco

Life Is a Gift

S o many people I know are riddled with regret. It seems they are always hung up on what they could have done or should have done. I think this causes undue stress, and stress is a real killer. I've always tried to take any struggles or mishaps as life lessons and apply them to who I am at the moment, and to who I want to be in the future. In other words, these times of hardship are the events that can make us better people moving forward.

We all tend to take things for granted, so I strive to live each moment as if it's my last. That way I eliminate the possibility of having regrets. We are put on this planet for only a certain amount of time, and then in a flash, it's over—so I feel it's best to always make the most of the gifts that we have been given. There are miracles around us all the time; all you need to do is take chances and experience what life has to offer. Yes, we all make mistakes, but it's not where you start that matters; it's where you end up.

Having lived through the Depression, I count my blessings every day for the fact that I've wound up with such a successful career. When my father died, my mother had to work like a slave doing piecework for a penny a dress as a seamstress, in order to put food on the table for her three children. Everyone in our neighborhood was very poor back then, so we were all in the same boat. Even still, seeing my mother struggling alone to support us made an indelible impression on me.

Coming from such humble beginnings and yet being able to achieve so much are in essence the American dream. What a magnificent gift I have been given to seek out truth and beauty through my art.

That being said, over the years I had to learn to be ready to receive the bounty that came my way; it's important to meet opportunity with preparedness. I was not always as prepared or open as I should have been. I was granted an amazing bonus early on in my singing career—but at times I didn't recognize when I was holding too hard a line. When Mitch Miller played me Hank Williams's hit "Cold, Cold Heart," I didn't think I should attempt to sing it; Hank's version was great, but it was so different from the kind of songs I did, with the country fiddling and his yodeling voice. "It's a good song, but I'm a city guy, and I wouldn't know how to sing something like that," I told Mitch.

Mitch objected strongly, declaring, "If I have to tie you to a tree, you're going to do it." He emphasized the beautiful words

I gave the Beatles their first major awards in 1965, and my first thought of Paul was that he had "it"—the star factor. *Steve Jennings*

The master of Zen—it was an honor to meet His Holiness, the Dalai Lama, at an event I attended in 2010 through the Gere Foundation with my daughter Johanna. *David Turnley*

I always have fun hanging around with Michael Bublé!

Courtesy of Sony Music Entertainment

John Legend is an exceptional composer and singer.

Reuben Cox

I love working and spending time with James Taylor.
He is a true gentleman. *Reuben Cox*

When I sang "Lullaby of Broadway" with the Dixie Chicks,
I thought they sounded just like the Andrews Sisters.

Reuben Cox

What a thrill to sing one of my all-time favorite songs, "Smile,"
with Barbra Streisand. *Courtesy of Sony Music Entertainment*

Diana Krall is a wonderful jazz musician—every time
I see her, she gets better and better. *Reuben Cox*

Jazz music has no bigger fan than Clint Eastwood—
and he composes his own music. *Adam Rose*

Michelle Obama *Barack Obama*

I was honored to be invited by the president and first lady
to sing at the White House at a tribute to Stevie Wonder.

Pete Souza/Official White House Photograph

Elton John is the ultimate professional—when we recorded
"Rags to Riches" for *Duets*, we did it in thirty-six minutes!

Reuben Cox

Recording with Lady Gaga was the most fun I have ever had in the studio.
She is a true artist, and she will be as big as Elvis Presley.

Kelsey Bennett

Willie Nelson has
a wonderful face—
I was glad to have a
chance to sketch him
when we recorded
together in Nashville.
Monroe Robertson

Nat King Cole would be so proud of his daughter Natalie—she is a
magnificent singer and a beautiful person. *Josh Cheuse*

Performing at the Metropolitan Opera, I loved having Aretha Franklin join me onstage for a duet. *Larry Busacca/Getty Images*

Josh Groban got a kick out of singing with just my jazz quartet, and not a symphony orchestra, when we recorded together. *Kelsey Bennett*

Amy Winehouse was one of a kind—an absolute genius.

Kelsey Bennett

I loved the fact that John Mayer wore a suit to our recording session— and he is a wonderful blues singer. *Courtesy of the author*

It was such fun to get to work with Robert De Niro when I did a cameo in the film *Analyze This*. *Larry Busacca/Getty Images*

One of my dearest friends, Harry Belafonte, with his lovely wife, Pam, visiting the Frank Sinatra School of the Arts. *Kelsey Bennett*

Susan and me on the opening day of the Frank Sinatra School of the Arts in 2009. The students there are fantastic—they give their all every day. *Gary Gershoff/Getty Images*

My beautiful wife, Susan, and our Teacup Maltese, Happy.

Rubén Martín

There is no better inspiration for art than studying nature.
Courtesy of the author

With Daegal and Danny, visiting our ancestral home,
Podargoni, in Calabria, Italy. *Kelsey Bennett*

In Calabria, Italy, re-creating the family legend that my
father would sing on the top of the mountain overlooking his village,
and that people at the foot of the mountain could hear him.

Kelsey Bennett

Seventeen Grammy Awards! I can hardly believe it!

Courtesy of the Recording Academy®/Danny Clinch © 2007

and melody, and after a while, he convinced me that I should try it. We made the record and the song hit the airwaves, starting out slowly. But then it caught on and climbed up the charts, and eventually it reached number one.

Back then there was no such thing as "crossover" music. It was either blues or country or jazz or pop; never country-rock or that sort of thing. But because of my putting out "Cold, Cold Heart," Hank's songs caught on everywhere. It was the first time a country tune had crossed over to the top-forty charts, and eventually it went on to be the first international country hit. We sold 2 million copies, and I'm sure he did well with it, too. One day Hank himself called me up and jokingly said, "Hey, what's the idea of ruining my song?" Later I was told that he would play my version of it when he was with friends, which made me feel wonderful.

And if you can believe it, I almost missed out on recording the career-defining "I Left My Heart in San Francisco."

George Cory and Douglass Cross were a songwriting team who lived in New York City. They were always pitching their new pieces to singers and musicians, trying to get them recorded. One day they ran into Ralph Sharon, my accompanist, and handed him a batch of sheet music. Ralph was so busy that he put it in a dresser drawer and forgot it was there.

Two years later, Ralph was packing to go to a concert we were doing in Hot Springs, Arkansas; from there we'd head to the Fairmont Hotel in San Francisco, where I'd never before performed. He was rummaging through his dresser for clothes to bring on the trip and came across the songs from Cory and Cross. Right on the top was "I Left My Heart in San Francisco." Since we were going to be playing there, he snatched it up along with his shirts.

We did our gig at the club in Hot Springs, where former president Bill Clinton later told me he watched our show through a window, since at the time he wasn't old enough to be admitted. After the show, Ralph and I went down to the hotel bar to run through some things, and he played "I Left My Heart" on the piano. I thought it was great, but what really clinched it was the bartender's reaction. "If you record that song, I promise I'll buy the very first copy," he said.

I'd heard that San Francisco audiences were a bit hard to warm up if they weren't familiar with your act, so I figured this song about their town might help. Marty Manning wrote a fantastic chart, and I sang it on the opening night at the Fairmont. The crowd absolutely loved it. That could have been all she wrote, but a Columbia rep heard it and thought the sales in San Francisco alone would make it a good idea to record it. I got it down in a single take, and Ralph called Cory and Cross, who were thrilled that I'd finally done one of their tunes.

In those days, you had an A side and a B side on records. The A side of this one was a song called "Once Upon a Time," and the B side was "I Left My Heart in San Francisco." The funny thing is, you never know how a song is going to do out in the world. You might think, *Oh, this one really has potential*, but you never know until it gets out there. So I was promoting

"Once Upon a Time" like anything for about six weeks, because it was the A side. The Columbia people called me up and said, "Turn it over and plug the San Francisco side; it's selling like hotcakes." I did, and I guess the rest is history.

"I Left My Heart" sold thousands and thousands of copies every week for the next several years, and it became the biggest song of my whole career. People in San Francisco treat me like a king when I'm in town, and the Fairmont Hotel just gave me the top suite, which they're calling the Tony Bennett Suite; they've even put some of my artwork in there. The B side of that record, "Once Upon a Time," also became a trademark song of mine, and I've always loved performing it onstage.

"I Left My Heart in San Francisco" was my first gold record, and because of it, I won my first Grammy. I think one reason for its popularity is that the lyrics represent the fulfillment of a dream. There is one special place in life that embodies all that you feel and believe in, and it remains an anchor of sorts that reminds you of your values and what's deeply and permanently important. We'd all like to be successful someday; the lines about coming home to the city mean that the person's dream did come true. Often people ask me if I ever get tired of singing it, since it's a standard part of my repertoire. I always reply, "Do you ever get tired of making love?"

———————

Several times in my life I've benefited purely by chance. In the mid-sixties, I was working the Hollywood Bowl with Count

Basie, with Buddy Rich on drums. There must have been eighteen thousand people there. I was in the middle of singing "Lost in the Stars," a Kurt Weill song, when all of a sudden the whole audience let out a gasp and a "Wow!" I thought maybe I'd hit a particularly strong note or something. But when I came offstage and asked why they did that, a crew member said, "Didn't you see what happened? When you were singing the song, a shooting star fell over the Bowl. It was incredible."

The next morning I got a call from Ray Charles, who was in New York. I said, "Good morning, Ray," and he said, "How'd you do that?" Later on we became good friends, and he always reminded me of the shooting star that fate handed me.

Sometimes life hands you gifts like that shooting star, and I am also a firm believer that karma has something to do with moments like that: what goes around in life tends to come back around. This has certainly been true for me a number of times. When I first started making it in the business, I was hanging out with a guy I was friendly with, Dave Victorson, who told me, "I'm flat broke. I want to go to L.A. and try my luck there, but I don't have a cent to my name." I asked him how much it would take, and he said five hundred dollars. I gave it to him, to help him out—and then I forgot all about it.

Some seven years later, Dave called me out of the blue. "You're coming to work for me," he said.

"What do you mean?" I asked.

Dave told me he'd just been named the entertainment director for a new Vegas hotel. He always remembered my loaning him the money, and he ended up paying me back a thousand-fold by booking me regularly at what turned out to be Caesars Palace. I wound up having a lifetime contract there.

I've seen this kind of thing over and over: someone does someone else a favor, not expecting anything back, and at a point in time—whether it's a month later, or several years in the making—the favor is repaid. It's yet another way in which life rewards us. It definitely pays to be kind.

———————

Throughout my career, audiences have been amazing to me. The fact that I can still perform to full houses internationally is a great privilege, and my relationship with the people of Great Britain has been particularly enriching. I've always had a fantastic time in that country, and I've been performing there for over fifty years. One especially nice trait about the people of England is that once they know you, you become part of their family. It's very unusual; you never go out of style, because they're so loyal. Then that generation grows up, and their children wind up coming to see you, too. Every time I go there, it's a real treat to put on a show for them.

I've done seven command performances in London, and each one was incredibly special. There is a protocol; the royalty sits on the left in the balcony at the Palladium, and you're not allowed to look at that box. Instead, you sing to the proscenium audience. At the end of the concert, traditionally you turn to the box and bow to the queen.

I was present in the fifties when Jack Benny was the closing artist at one of these performances. He came out at eleven at night, looked out at the audience, and then up toward the queen and said directly to her, "They told me to be here at eight." I'll tell you, I never heard a bigger laugh from an audience in my life. He changed the whole history of Britain with that one line; everyone left the place chuckling.

Playing at the one hundredth anniversary of Royal Albert Hall in 1971 was something else. We had the London Philharmonic Orchestra as well as fifteen fantastic British jazz artists onstage, and I performed a lot of classic pieces and many of my big hits to that date. The concert sold out, and the audience seemed to love every minute of it. NBC showed a tape of the concert in the United States and it got very strong ratings. It was another high point in a career that has handed me many gifts.

———

So many people look at life with regret instead of joy. They're tired, angry, or bigoted—but that's such a waste of time. I wish I could take all of those individuals and help them feel good or hopeful about themselves; I try to achieve this through my show. It's my wish that everyone in the audience can pick up something from a song, or a moment in the show, that becomes unforgettable to them. If I can make them feel that, then I'm repaying some of the rewards that I've received.

I feel that what I do for a living is a very noble job; I'm on a journey to communicate how beautiful our daily experience can be. Life is a gift, and we should all cherish it. It's as simple as that.

The Zen of Bennett

Be ready to recognize the gifts of life when they arrive at your doorstep.

Remember that what goes around comes around. If you are good to someone, at some point in time that act of kindness will come back to you.

Sometimes gifts arrive in the form of a happy accident. Be prepared to accept these rewards.

Being angry is a waste of time. Instead, count your blessings every day.

Make a real effort to appreciate the gifts that life has given you.

Inn on the Park
London England

London

Citizen of the World

When I was young, one of my uncles arrived in New York from his native Italy. He was so taken by the welcome he received that he sewed together an oversized flag that combined the American flag with various other flags from around the world, and he hung it outside his house. This small token of appreciation predated the United Nations, but he didn't realize that it was against the law to deface the American flag. The police came to his house and threatened to arrest him if he didn't take it down. My uncle didn't speak English, so at first he was very confused. But the point was made to him loud and clear, so he removed it.

Even so, America really was the melting pot that it promised to be for new arrivals from other countries. In fact, the United States still represents a world without borders. This country's diversity has inspired me to appreciate the fact that people everywhere have each other in common; we truly are all neighbors.

Ella Fitzgerald used to say something to me over and over that drove home this very point. With this incredible warmth in her eyes, Ella would say, "Tony, we're all here . . ." What she meant by this statement was that on this little planet called Earth, we're not Italians, we're not Jewish, Christian, or Catholic; instead, we're all here together. That we are all really citizens of the world. And to me, that completely sums it up. We only live a short time; only a brief ninety or a hundred years at most, and that really goes by quickly. In order to appreciate the gifts we've been given, we need to learn the beauty of just being alive, and of being good to one another. That's a big lesson that many of us haven't yet embraced. We need to start putting down the greed and the racism. People who think, *I've got mine; the hell with everybody else*, aren't contributing anything to society. You have to think in a more all-encompassing way and say, "Is this good for all of us on the planet?" It's amazing to me that so many people still don't realize this. If the human race is going to survive, we need to figure out how to get along. We Americans live in such a great country; it's the first place where people of every nationality and every religion were allowed to live together. That's one reason why America is great; we have so many philosophies to draw from here, and therefore we have a lot more to work with than other countries do. We need to accentuate this more, both in our schools and in society.

Life Is a Gift

On Thanksgiving in 1945, I was in Mannheim, Germany, as part of the occupying American Army. The whole place had been demolished during the war by our bombers. I was walking around and by an amazing coincidence, I ran into my old buddy Frank Smith, a fellow serviceman who had played drums in our group in high school. I couldn't believe I'd run into Frank over there. I was so happy to see a familiar face from back home, after fighting on the front line and being surrounded by strangers for so long. Frank took me with him to a service at a Baptist church, and then because I was allowed to invite one guest for the army's Thanksgiving dinner in the mess hall, I asked him to join me.

When we got to the hall, a red-faced officer came up to me in a fury and screamed, "Get your gear, you're out of here! I don't like the people you associate with." "Are you serious?" I asked. "He's my friend from school." But the officer just said, "I don't care where he's from. Get out." He took a razor from his pocket and cut my stripes from my shirt, threw them on the ground, and told me I was no longer a corporal; I was being demoted to a private. For a minute I didn't comprehend why he was doing this, but then I realized it was because Frank was African American, and therefore he wasn't allowed in the segregated mess hall.

This was just unbelievable to me, even though I knew that

prejudice was common in the Army back then. At that time, African Americans had to have their own barracks, bars, and everything. The Army actually felt that it was better to fraternize with the Germans than it was to be friends with a black man from our own country! I hadn't been brought up that way, so it was a shock when the officer treated us so badly. Not only did we not get our Thanksgiving dinner, I was then put on graves registration duty. This meant that I had to dig up the bodies of soldiers who hadn't been properly buried on the battlefields, and rebury them in individual graves. It was the most sad and depressing job I've ever had to do.

That day is seared upon my memory; I've thought about it often. We were just two homesick kids glad to see a familiar face, but for the Army, the only thing that mattered was the color of our skin.

Luckily, after a few weeks on grave duty, through the efforts of a friend, Major Letkoff, I was able to get reassigned to the radio network in Wiesbaden. But that incident with Frank Smith shaped my opinions forever. I had grown up listening to brilliant African American artists such as Art Tatum, Louis Armstrong, Duke Ellington, Ella Fitzgerald, and Dinah Washington; when I got to know them later on, they all were kind and generous to a fault. So where was the rationale for such bigotry?

During the fifties, when I was starting out, I ran into many instances of racism when I worked with African American musicians. Even a genius like Nat King Cole was discriminated against. Once I went to see Nat perform in Miami, and I invited him to join my table afterward. He told me that he wasn't allowed in the dining room, so I'd have to visit him backstage if I wanted to see him. That kind of Jim Crow law revolted me; I just didn't understand it. But these restrictions were the order of the day.

Natalie Cole and I spoke recently about the fact that even though he was up against these bigoted attitudes, her father's multimillion-dollar record sales enabled the record company to construct the whole building for Capitol Records. It's literally known as "the House That Nat Built." People were listening to his music all over America and loving it, but in certain places the man who made the music and who made a lot of people a lot of money wasn't allowed to eat in the same dining room as those he performed for—an absolute travesty.

When the Americana Hotel opened in Miami in the mid-fifties, Duke Ellington and I were performing there, but Duke wasn't allowed to come to the press party afterward. He and his band couldn't stay at the hotel, either; they had to lodge in a run-down joint in another part of town.

Nat and Duke were brilliant human beings who gave the world some of the most beautiful music ever made, yet they were treated like second-class citizens. The whole thing made me furious. When Harry Belafonte called me in 1965 and asked me to join Martin Luther King's civil rights march from Selma to Montgomery, Alabama, he described to me what had been happening in the South. "It's genocide," he told me. "They're doing horrible things to black people; there's great injustice."

It was so awful that it took me only a couple of minutes to say, "I'm coming with you."

Harry told me that earlier that month, Dr. King and the organizers had tried to march from Selma to Montgomery in support of voting rights, and that they were planning a third march. Dr. King wanted some celebrities along to attract the public's attention and to entertain the marchers. Among others who came out were Leonard Bernstein, Sammy Davis Jr., and Shelley Winters.

The march began the week of March 21, and the police, all white, were extremely hostile; it reminded me of the Army's attitude when I tried to bring my friend Frank to Thanksgiving dinner. Violence was a daily reality in the civil rights era, and as we headed out from Selma, jazz singer Billy Eckstine and I were very frightened. Fortunately, Harry reassured everyone on the route and kept the marchers calm.

On the evening of the twenty-fourth, the march organizers put together a rally called "Stars for Freedom," in which all the performers put on a show. I sang a few songs, as did Harry Belafonte; Sammy Davis Jr.; Peter, Paul, and Mary; Frankie Laine; and Nina Simone. No stage was around, so ironically a local mortician brought a bunch of wooden coffins with which they built a platform. It was surreal to perform on a stack of coffins, but we did what we had to.

On Thursday, March 25, twenty-five thousand people marched to the steps of the state capitol, where King delivered the speech "How Long, Not Long." When the march was over, we were all held up in a "safe house," and various volunteers drove people to the airport or back to their homes. When it came time for Billy Eckstine and me to head out, we gave up our seats to others. We later found out that the driver was assassinated by the Ku Klux Klan on her way back. She was Viola Liuzzo, a white mother of five from Detroit who had come to Alabama to give her support. It was a horrendous tragedy that saddened us no end.

But the physical danger didn't keep droves of people from coming out to support the effort, and the entire country was forced to take note. I have always felt proud to have been part of such a historic event, one that helped to change society's views of African Americans and their struggle for equality, in the South and elsewhere.

Aretha Franklin recently gave me a letter that acknowledged my role in the movement:

Hi Tony,

A note to say thank you for the most absolutely gorgeous flowers on both occasions, and to applaud your humanity in the civil rights movement with Dr. King in the 1960s. Looking forward to keeping the music playing together.

All the best,

Aretha

Her comments made me feel very proud.

I was determined to perform with only the top musicians wherever I went, regardless of race, creed, or color. That's how I was brought up—to believe in the fundamental American principle that all people are created equal and should be treated as such. As hard as it is to fathom, I was the first white performer to sing with Count Bill Basie. I insisted on having him alongside me at the Copacabana in New York; prior to that, they didn't allow black musicians to set foot inside. Later, when Basie and I played a show at the Philadelphia Academy of Music, we were on first and the audience went wild. Joe Williams was singing, and the Basie band was smoking—we "wiped out the theater and greased up the walls," as Basie put it. On top of that, we received ten standing ovations.

After the show, Basie and I were out in the parking lot commenting on how it had gone. "What an audience; wasn't that great?" This white guy came up to Basie, threw him his keys, and said, "Hey, get me my car, will you?" He assumed that Bill was the parking attendant. "Get your own car," Bill replied. "I've been parking them all night." Even faced with that kind of bigotry, he still kept his dignity and sense of humor.

When I did a series of concerts in the mid-seventies with Lena Horne, whom I adored, the only thing that clouded the good vibes was this kind of bigotry. Lena was such a class act, a great lady with an incredible work ethic. We sang Harold Arlen songs that had been arranged as duets for us, and later both Cary Grant and Fred Astaire separately told me that the concert with Lena was the best show they'd ever seen in their lives. We went all over the place doing that show, and I loved it. Arlen's songs are great for a jazz singer like me; you can do them as they were written or with your own interpretation, and any treatment works fine. Harold always said he loved improvisation; he'd tell me to change a song the way I wanted to. As long as the audience was happy, he was fine with what you did. And Lena and I had a magnificent time doing them as duets.

During rehearsals, we saw our managers talking in the wings. "I know what they're saying," Lena said. "They're going to tell us to walk offstage in different directions, so it won't seem as if we're leaving together." And sure enough, that's what they told us to do. We could perform together, but we couldn't appear to be friends or to be hanging out.

It was shocking to me how much prejudice there was, even in Hollywood; blacks and whites just weren't allowed to get along, which was so ridiculous. Thank goodness some progress has been made since those days. I don't think anyone back then could imagine that we would ever have an African American president and first lady in the White House. That fact alone makes me proud to be an American, and happy that we as a country are truly becoming citizens of the world.

It's funny; sometimes when people who are well-off ask me where I'm from and I say Astoria, they laugh at me because it's so down compared to the big skyscrapers in Manhattan. That's really another form of prejudice. But I secretly laugh back at them, because I know that the greatest part of New York City is Astoria, since it's where the secretaries, the teachers, the writers, the promising actors and actresses and directors live. Before they become famous, many of them start out there—as do the firemen and the policemen; everyone who makes the whole city work. You name it, they run it—and they take great pride in doing things right. And I loved growing up there.

You'll find any country that you've ever been to represented in New York City. It's a fabulous cultural center. There's no place like it anywhere else, because you have a cross section of the entire world right here.

I believe it was my upbringing in such a culturally diverse place that has allowed me to connect to audiences all around the world. The classic songs of the Great American Songbook unite us all, regardless of class, color, or citizenship, and by performing them for people in other countries, I'm able to build relations with audiences everywhere—and I do mean everywhere.

Recording the duets albums brought me to many locations around the world as well. It was a thrill to be back in London to record "Body and Soul" with Amy Winehouse. We recorded it at the famous Abbey Road Studios, where artists like the Beatles and the London Symphony Orchestra had done some of their best work. Amy had never been to the studio, and she loved the whole setup, as I did. When I went to record with Andrea Bocelli, I went to his home in Pisa. He was so gracious, and served a fantastic Italian meal for the whole crew. The entire process was an unforgettable journey.

But when I initially started touring internationally, I had some groundwork to do. When I first went to Rio de Janeiro, I wasn't well known at all. So when I performed in the original Copacabana in Rio, a beautiful hotel right on the beach, I played to maybe fifteen people a night. Even though the audience was sparse, I knocked myself out to communicate to them, and they all stayed until my show was over. Every evening, despite the small crowd, I gave it 200 percent; and every night, there would be only ten or so people in the seats.

The funny thing is, over the years, I've run into *hundreds* of people who tell me that they saw me at the Copacabana doing those performances. I think word of mouth got out that something special happened at those shows, and others wanted to claim they were there, too. But they couldn't have been, because those audiences were so tiny. Yet through the years it keeps building. Today I get rave reviews and packed crowds, and I love the Brazilian people—they're warm and welcoming.

In 2007, the United Nations gave me its Citizen of the World Award, and I received the Martin Luther King Salute to Greatness Award for my efforts against discrimination. It was a proud moment for me. But perhaps one of the best moments was when Stevie Wonder presented me with the Billboard Century Award. "My friend Tony Bennett had been there for my people early on, earlier than most, and has stayed the course ever since," Stevie said in presenting me with the award. "He has helped demand the social, economic, and civil rights of every American. I grew up hearing his music and his name in my household." As much as anything, that made me feel like a true citizen of the world.

I strongly believe that we must dedicate our lives to world peace and to putting down hatred. All people want is to be let alone to live their lives, in a place where their children can grow up free of fear and tyranny. It's the greatest gift that we can leave for future generations.

The Zen of Bennett

In reality, we are not Italian, Jewish, Christian, or Catholic; instead, we are all citizens of the world.

In order to appreciate the gifts we've been given, we need to learn the beauty of being alive, and of being good to one another.

Before we do something, we need to ask ourselves, Is this good for all of us on the planet?

Citizens of all nations need to figure out how to get along; it's the only way the human race is going to survive.

If we can learn to embrace some of our differences and coexist, everyone on the planet will benefit.

Self-Portrait

Sometimes Turn Off All the Mics

I'm all for keeping things simple. I like to say that if you can't explain yourself in sixteen minutes, you should go back to the drawing board. The preferred venues today seem to be arenas or stadiums. There are always a lot of lights, fireworks, and dancers crowding the stage. I don't understand how you keep in touch with your audience that way; I prefer beautiful concert halls with excellent acoustics.

America has some of the best halls in the world: Carnegie Hall and Radio City in New York, and Heinz Hall in Pittsburgh. Then there are the Fox theaters in Atlanta and St. Louis, which were gorgeous old vaudeville houses—just to name a few. I love to perform where I can see whom I'm singing to; it's much more intimate. Technology is wonderful when it's used correctly, but if you don't have the talent to back it up and you have to rely on bells and whistles, then it all becomes smoke and mirrors.

I'm a big believer in standing on your own two feet without a lot of artifice, and I am inspired by others who believe the same. Once when Maurice Chevalier was performing at the Waldorf-Astoria hotel in New York, there was a musicians' strike. Instead of canceling the show, Chevalier walked onto the stage all alone and sang the entire thing a cappella. The audience loved it, and he wound up getting six standing ovations. If that's not self-reliance, I don't know what is.

I always remembered that story, and I worked the idea into my own act. Near the end of my show, I ask my longtime soundman, Tom Young, to turn off all the microphones, and I sing with only the acoustics of the concert hall and without any amplification. People always tend to remember that portion of my show; it leaves quite an impression.

In a way, singing without a mic is an example of taking responsibility for myself and having faith in myself as a performer. There's nothing artificial affecting my voice; it's just me belting it out to the audience and hitting the back of the hall. When we put ourselves out there—whether it's auditioning for a record label or interviewing for a job—we have to know how to stand on our own two feet and believe in ourselves. There won't always be a mic, or other musicians, or a crowd to fall back on. You have to be able to rely on yourself alone, at crucial times in your life.

Such was the case at age eighteen, when I got drafted into the Army. I'd never been away from home except for a brief time with my relatives upstate when my father died, so heading into basic military training was quite a shock. I was sent to Fort Dix, New Jersey, and then on to Little Rock, Arkansas, for six weeks, to prepare before heading to Europe to join the fighting.

Boot camp was much worse than I could have imagined. I was in the infantry rifleman division, and it was very rough. We had to go on seemingly endless marches through brambles and mud, and the officers tried to break our spirits. The whole military philosophy went against everything I was raised to believe in, and the institutionalized bigotry in the Army disgusted me.

Ironically, given that I wound up being a singer, the sergeant was always on me about not being able to keep time when I was marching. Once when we were on a bivouac mission, he began yelling at me and hitting my helmet with his crop. I'd had all I could take; I turned on my heel and walked the six miles back to camp. As punishment, I was put on kitchen duty for a month. I also had to clean the whole unit's Browning rifles, which got filthy from the gunpowder when they were fired. It took almost an hour to clean one hammer, and I had to do a dozen or so at a time. On top of that, I was stuck working every weekend, instead of being able to take a little R and R with the other guys.

Finally I got to go on leave, and when I arrived home in Queens, I dropped onto the floor in a dead faint. The abusive environment in boot camp, combined with my emotional state, overcame me. A few days later I had to go back, and when the training was over, I went home for a short while, and then was called up with a group of troops bound for Germany.

Instead of replacing an entire division of soldiers when it

became exhausted, the way the German and British armies did, the American Army would substitute an individual soldier in a unit when someone became unable to fight. Many of these new guys had never even fired a gun. The idea was that the veteran soldiers would teach them, but it didn't work that way, and the whole setup was a disaster.

I was shipped out to Le Havre, France, and then to a holding area. None of us knew each other, since we'd all been pulled from different divisions, so it was a time when I really had to go it alone. There was no chance to make friends, because in a few days, I would be shipped out with yet another group of strangers to the front lines. This system, which was called "repple depple" (the soldiers' term for *replacement depot*), was impersonal and very lonely. We were a bunch of eighteen- to twenty-year-olds who had been plucked from our homes and families and suddenly put into this terrifying situation without even a friend to lean on.

The American Army had suffered so many casualties that they just needed to keep a flow of young men through the troops to fill up the depleted divisions, no matter how little the new guys knew about combat. Over half of the new soldiers died within the first week on the front line. I was assigned to the Seventh Army, 63rd Infantry Division of the 255th Regiment, G Company. I was put into an Army truck and sent across France during January and February 1945. In March we entered Germany and went straight to the front line. Nothing could have prepared me for what was to come next.

The Battle of the Bulge had just ended in France, and the German army was retreating. Even so, Hitler sent his troops to the Ardennes to try to keep the Americans from occupying his country. When the Allies broke through and went into Germany, I was one of the replacements for the exhausted American soldiers.

The veterans returning from the front acted as if they would rather have died instead of losing their friends, and as I said earlier, I really felt their sadness. The winter was freezing, and being at the front was unbearable. Bombers flew overhead, and shells burst all around us. Fellow soldiers died right before my eyes. I wondered when it would be my turn.

The real horror was the German cannons. We had to dig foxholes before we went to sleep, and sometimes it took forever to break through the frozen ground. You'd eat ice-cold cheese and crackers, pass out for a couple of hours, and then you had to get up again. Talk about being thrown back on your own resources. On my very first night on the line, I was so tired after digging my hole that I fell asleep on the ground next to it. I woke up covered in snow, and right behind me there was a tree trunk with a big piece of shrapnel stuck into it. A few inches lower, and it would have hit me.

The nights were the worst. It was bitter cold, but we couldn't light a fire to stay warm because the Germans would see it. We'd spend up to sixteen hours lying alone in a foxhole, listening for the enemy. Sometimes we could even hear them talking to each other, they were so close.

Eventually I made it off of the front line and wound up working for the Special Services Band, which was a great experience after the battlefield. But being on the front was definitely a lesson in self-reliance.

It isn't only traumatic events that help one practice keeping things centered. Painting does that for me in a big way, since I'm all by myself when I'm in my studio. It's definitely not a board meeting; it's not six guys making a group decision. When you're at the canvas, you're all alone, and you're thinking about your own story. Just you—not your friends, your wife and family. I find that painting brings me back to myself in a way that makes me aware that in the end, all we really can rely on is ourselves.

It's similar to performing. The thing about putting on a show is that, although it takes all the people around you to make sure it comes off the way you want it to—the soundmen, the lighting people, the guy who raises the curtain—I'm also aware that it's really all on my shoulders. It's me out there again on the front line. When the audience reacts and the reviews hit the street the next morning, it all reflects on me. It's wonderful and important to be surrounded by people who care about and support you, but when it really comes down to it, we come into and exit this world alone. I've worked very hard to be self-reliant, to learn to believe in myself, and to embrace each waking day with confidence that I will be able to accomplish the things I set out to do.

The Zen of Bennett

There won't always be a mic, or other musicians, or a crowd to fall back on.

The art of painting teaches you who you are. When you're at the canvas, you're all alone; you're thinking about your own story.

In the end, all we really can rely on is ourselves.

Be determined to stay the course and stand on your own two feet.

Bill Evans

Go with Truth and Beauty

T here are so many wonderful things to say about my profession. The people I meet; the events I've experienced; the museums; the concerts, all have afforded me the opportunity to keep learning, and to keep growing into the person I strive to be. But there is a very tragic side to the entertainment business, and it can't be ignored. I've known some of the best in the business who have been swallowed up by the pressure to perform at their peak all the time, while being under harsh constant public scrutiny. There are many pitfalls and hazards along the way; if you aren't careful, they can sneak up on you, grab hold, and never let go.

The life of an entertainer might seem glamorous, and it has its moments—but it isn't always that way. Although many aspects of life as an entertainer are very exciting, there is also a lot of downtime traveling and waiting to hit the stage. "Hurry up and wait" is a phrase that I like to throw around. The pressure is always on to hurry up and get to where you are going, but by the time you get there, you end up waiting for what seems like intolerable amounts of time. Cary Grant cited boredom as a major reason why I should avoid the movie business and stick to singing when I asked him for his advice on my future in film. It was also the reason why he retired from his screen career. As I mentioned earlier, he told me that he spent half of his life in trailers on a studio lot and on location. "Tony, that's no life at all," he added. At a certain point, he just left it all behind and put his energies into enjoying himself.

Unfortunately it's when that boredom sets in that many entertainers turn to drugs or alcohol to fill up the time. They take pills to stay up, and then pills to go to sleep. It can be very easy to slip into this pattern and extremely difficult to get out of it. There have been times throughout my life that I fell victim to drugs, but fortunately I had the wherewithal to come to my senses. I am forever grateful that I did. I stay healthy, work out, try to learn something new every day, and never get bored. But many of my dear friends weren't as lucky.

Noted film producer and manager Jack Rollins, who worked as Woody Allen's manager and was my manager for a brief time in the seventies, told me that the comedian Lenny Bruce "sinned against his talent." (That sentence changed my life. From that moment on, I stopped taking all drugs and got myself back in top shape.) What Jack was talking about was the fact that Bruce ruined his life and career by taking drugs. Rol-

lins's statement about sinning against one's talent really resonated with me because I've had several good friends who were
addicted. One was the legendary Bill Evans, who is considered
by many to be the most influential postwar jazz pianist. Bill
and I put out two records in the seventies, and as I described
earlier, it was some of the best work I'd ever done.

I first met Bill in 1962, when I sang with Dave Brubeck at
a White House concert. Bill had played with the Miles Davis
Sextet and later had his own trio. He was the best-known jazz
pianist in the world, so I was excited about the idea of working
with him.

Bill and I really hit it off. We didn't want anyone to distract
us when we were recording, so we had just one engineer and
Bill's manager with us in the studio. I would suggest a tune, Bill
would find a key, and we'd work it out together. The experience
was so intense; we did nine songs in the first three days. I told
the engineer not to wait for us to do a take; just to keep the tape
running all the time, so we didn't miss anything—but he said
he would run out of tape if he did that. To this day, I wished
we had recorded all the run-throughs. Later on, Bill said that
working with me was one of the prime experiences of his life,
which meant quite a lot to me.

The sad thing was, Bill was addicted to heroin. He said to
me, "It's the worst thing that ever happened to me. I need to
shoot up just to feel okay." He was a genius, and yet it was so
hard for him to beat that stuff. He always told me, "I wish I
would have knocked out the first person who stuck a needle in

my arm." He needed to have a shot just to feel normal. It was such a pity that he never could get over the habit. Yet even in the throes of his addiction, no one else has ever played piano like that. He was so good that when he played with a symphony, he sounded better than the entire orchestra.

Right before Bill died, he called me from a little town near Akron, Ohio, where he was working. "Tony, I want to tell you one thing: just go with truth and beauty, and forget everything else," he told me. "Just do that." Ever since then, truth and beauty have been the essence of what it's all about for me.

Judy Garland was another close friend who never had a chance. She was incredibly talented, and such a beautiful person. Judy grew up in the film studio, signing with Metro-Goldwyn-Mayer as a young teenager. They had her cranking out a movie every six weeks; the pressure was intense, and they started pumping her with pills at a very early age. She was also exposed to the underbelly of the business, which meant that she had to grow up pretty quickly. On top of that, she was very insecure about her looks. Everything was managed for her, and most of her money was ripped off in the typical Hollywood style, leaving her with massive debts that became impossible for her to handle. Unfortunately, she died at only forty-seven years of age. To me, she was the most intelligent person in Hollywood.

More recently, one person I wish I'd been able to help was Amy Winehouse. Amy had thanked me for my influence in the liner notes of her first album, long before we'd even met. I also gave Amy her first Grammy Award when she won for Best New

Artist in 2008. She came to three of my shows when I was in London—two at Royal Albert Hall, and one in Camden—and I had a chance to meet her and her family face-to-face. Later, she told me that seeing me at Albert Hall those evenings were two of the best nights of her and her father's life. Later that year I invited her to sing with me on my second duets record. I was thrilled when she agreed, and we decided that she would perform "Body and Soul" with me. Sadly, it wound up being the last song she ever recorded.

Amy said that "Body and Soul" was her father Mitch's favorite song in all the world. When Mitch heard what song we would be singing and asked Amy if she knew it, she told him, "Of course I know it; I'm your daughter." It's a great classic by Johnny Greene, and she was singing true jazz on the day we did it. Amy told me that she first began with jazz guitar and that she learned to sing by listening to jazz artists.

For the most part, contemporary musicians have listened to rock all their lives, but then along came Amy, who had such an innate sense and feeling for jazz.

When Amy came to record with me, she was a bit nervous at first because she wanted to get everything exactly right. She told me that she wasn't a natural-born performer, and that she got quite shy onstage. To relax her a bit, I mentioned Dinah Washington, and when Amy told me she was her favorite singer of all time, I told her that Dinah had been a good friend of mine. Amy was excited to hear that and asked me to tell her all about her.

I told her that Dinah used to come in to the entertainment director's office at Caesars Palace in Vegas without even having a booking; just with two suitcases in her hands. She'd come in and put the luggage down and say, "I'm here, boss." He'd tell her, "All right, go to work," and she'd stay as long as she wanted.

Dinah would go out and sing, and the club would be jammed. It was just word of mouth; no publicity or anything. She would stay up until ten o'clock the next morning, and then she'd ask, "What's everyone going to bed for?" After I had told her these stories, Amy commented on the fact that Dinah died so young, before age forty, and at the time we touched lightly on the fact that Dinah had had a rough life.

Amy was truly one of the best artists I've ever known. She was entirely sober, focused, and professional the day we recorded "Body and Soul." She was also a very spontaneous singer; she knew how to be in the moment. I sensed that in every note she sang, and I was knocked out by her voice; she was such a talent.

Everybody in Britain was rooting for Amy. She'd had a tough time with alcohol and substance abuse. I knew she had managed to get clean, but I was going to try to talk to her about it, since it's so easy to slip back into bad things. She seemed very impressed with me, so I was going to tell her to keep a clear head and slow down.

Unfortunately, I never got a chance to do that. I was going to have her on the show with me when I did the Palladium for my eighty-fifth birthday in London. When she died, four months to the day after our recording date, she was just twenty-seven.

I was on the road, and when Danny called me and told me, I started crying; I couldn't believe it. After we recorded, I had told the BBC in London, "I want to talk to that girl because if she doesn't keep clean, it's going to kill her." That's the last thing I told them. She was a little angel; Amy was born to sing to us.

Billie Holiday was another great artist who succumbed to drug addiction. I had gotten to see her play with Duke many years earlier, and she was such an inspiration to me that eventually I dedicated a tribute album to her, called *Bennett on Holiday*. So many people only knew about the sad aspects of Billie's life, but on the record, I focused on the more upbeat songs such as "What a Little Moonlight Can Do" and "Laughing at Life." Bobby Tucker, Billie's pianist for some time, helped me choose the songs for the record, which also wound up winning a Grammy.

People like Dinah, Bill, Judy, Amy, Billie, and Whitney Houston all had a touch of genius in them, and yet they were hooked. The world lost a lot of great music when each of them died.

The Zen of Bennett

To take drugs is to sin against one's talent.

Go with truth and beauty, and forget everything else.

Susan

21

Giving Back

Being a popular performer in the public eye comes with much responsibility. All of your fans look up to you, and at times they will take what you say and what you do as examples of how they should conduct themselves. People often criticize entertainers for taking a political stance or a position on social issues. I think this attitude is completely off the mark. This great country of ours is built on the basic precept of the right to speak our minds. We often forget that the highest office one can attain under a republic is not president, congressperson, or Supreme Court justice, but that of citizen.

Each one of us has the right to voice our opinions. It's important to remember that our democracy is "of the people, by the people, and for the people." So I feel strongly that it is important for entertainers to use their popularity to further causes that help those who are less fortunate than we are. It keeps our world moral and strong. When you think how dedicated to world affairs people like George Clooney, Bono, and my dear friend Harry Belafonte are, you can't ignore the positive effect that this has had on society at large.

———————

I've always admired the fact that Winston Churchill kept the paintings of the National Gallery in Britain during World War II, instead of shipping them out of the country, despite the threat of bombing. "Hide them in caves and cellars, but not one painting will leave this island," he famously said. Churchill held strong beliefs about the importance of the arts in education, and to the morale of the entire country.

When I was in Chicago a while back, I saw an entire city block filled with all kinds of great art. I learned that the artists were all students of the Gallery 37 program. This is the inspiring art program of the nonprofit organization After School Matters, which was set up to expose teens to after-school activities in all areas of education. I learned that the students were commissioned to create all kinds of artwork, including murals and sculpture, and even got paid for it. I returned to New York and told my wife, Susan, who was a teacher at a public arts high school in New York City, about the Chicago program that encourages young artists to make a living even while they are studying their art.

Like Churchill, I believe in the power of art education to transform the lives and attitudes of others. It certainly has had an impact on the kids in Chicago. What if I could bring art to the younger generation through a school of my own? It has always been a central priority in my life to teach the younger generation the artistic values that have made me a successful artist. A school for the arts in Astoria, my old neighborhood, would help to accomplish just that.

Susan agreed that this was a great idea, so I called up Danny at his office and told him I wanted to start a school. I insisted that it be a public high school, so kids all over New York would have access to a top-of-the-line facility devoted to all of the arts. My first thought was to call my old friend Peter Vallone Sr., who was City Council Speaker, and who gave me my very first singing job in Queens. It was one of the great thrills of my life, on my seventy-fifth birthday, to get the news from Speaker Vallone on the steps of the Metropolitan Museum that the city had approved $70 million for our arts school.

Founding the school also gave me the opportunity to "give back" to one of my dearest friends and mentors: I named it Frank Sinatra School of the Arts. Hopefully this act emphasized to others the importance of being a mentor for the younger generation. I first learned this from Louis Armstrong, who always mentioned in interviews that his mentor was Bix Beiderbecke, a great white trumpet player with Paul Whiteman's orchestra. Just as Louis always gave credit to his mentor, I too wanted to give credit to mine—Frank Sinatra.

While Susan and I dreamed of opening a brand-new school, we didn't want to wait years for the construction of a new building to be completed, so the city provided us with a temporary site. We opened the Sinatra School in 2001 with both former governor Mario Cuomo and Harry Belafonte on hand for opening day (two gentlemen who are also experts in "giving back").

The school flourished, and we began an intensive process to raise funds for our future permanent site while providing ongoing programmatic support. I was a product of public schools with quality arts programs, and Susan was a teacher at a public high school, so we understood that the arts could drive good academic performance. We also wanted to show the private sector how important it is to support the public school system, particularly since funding for the arts has been cut nationwide. We hoped our facility would become a blueprint for schools across the nation, so Susan and I also founded the nonprofit organization Exploring the Arts (ETA) in 1999 to help support arts programs in other public high schools.

We were very encouraged early on when I was asked to address the United States Conference of Mayors, who were meeting in Washington, D.C. I said that the Sinatra School was a model for what all other schools in the country should aim to become. Our initial focus was on the school's permanent site, and I wanted to make sure it would be a state-of-the-art facility with an incomparable concert hall, light-filled art studios, and beautiful dance rooms. Through our dear friend the philanthropist Iris Cantor, I had met the renowned architect James Polshek, who had designed many beautiful buildings and structures, including the Rose Center for Earth and Space at the

American Museum of Natural History, the William J. Clinton Presidential Library, and the Iris and B. Gerald Cantor Center for Visual Arts at Stanford University. Everyone said we would never get a world-class architectural firm such as Polshek to design our building, but I went to the firm directly and told them what Susan and I were trying to accomplish, and they immediately came on board.

In 2009, just a few blocks away from where I grew up in Astoria, at the Kaufman Astoria Studios complex and across the street from the Museum of the Moving Image, we christened the permanent site of the Frank Sinatra School of the Arts. We held an opening ceremony on the first day of school, and it was poignant for us all to have Frank's daughter Nancy and his granddaughter A.J. join us for the occasion.

I'm proud that we have raised millions in support of the Frank Sinatra School of the Arts. Ten years later, we now support arts programs in thirteen additional New York City public high schools. It was my dream as well to teach young artists how to perform and to have a good foundation that includes the rudiments of entertainment. To have this come true is unbelievable—right in my own hometown.

Studies have shown that students with high arts involvement perform better in school, do more community service activities, and have higher graduation rates, so it's very important for kids to be involved in the arts—from drama, dance, vocals, and instrumental music to film and fine arts.

Through ETA, we help public high schools create and sustain quality arts programs by providing critical equipment and supplies, funding artistic residencies, supporting scholarships, and funding professional development for teachers. I am very proud that our internship program places our students with the city's top arts institutions, which help prepare them for college and their careers. A majority of the students qualify for school lunches, and in the eleven years since the Sinatra School has been open, the percentage of its students living below the poverty level has doubled. Nearly 70 percent of all the kids in our partner schools live in poverty, so giving back to public education is essential. Most important is that the kids are getting an extensive and rich experience that makes them better artists, and which I feel also makes them better citizens of the world.

The students love attending the Sinatra School, and their parents often tell us, "You don't know what you did for my child; it's a new life." The program has rigorous academics as well as arts instruction; you teach the kids what the masters did, so they can learn. And we have seen firsthand that if you emphasize the arts in school, the kids like to come to class, so our attendance rates are terrific.

Over the years, we have had some of the highest graduation rates and percentages of kids going off to college—not only by New York City standards, but nationwide, with an average graduation rate of 95 percent and 85 percent going on to a four-year college. By the time our students leave the Sinatra School, they have had unique experiences: they've sung in places such as the United Nations headquarters, Carnegie Hall, and Radio

City Music Hall. We get them out in public so they understand what it will be like to perform after they've graduated. At many of ETA's partner schools, we support kids who are the first in their families to go on to college; the arts are a powerful and important part of their education. Our dream is to have quality arts programs in public high schools throughout the United States.

I know that many of my friends and colleagues thought it was ambitious—maybe too ambitious—to try to start a public school in New York City when I was at a point in my seventies when I could just sit back and relax. But I have learned that when you start giving back, you aren't alone. My son Danny, and a great many of my dear friends—Mario Cuomo, Harry Belafonte, Herb and Jeanne Siegel, Alec Baldwin, Elton John, and countless heads of corporations, as well as many generous private individuals—have joined Susan and me to promote the mission of Exploring the Arts.

I was backstage with President Obama at a concert in Washington when I told him about ETA. He was very supportive, and the very next day, he personally arranged for us to meet with Secretary of Education Arne Duncan. I was encouraged recently to hear that the President's Committee on the Arts and the Humanities has established a program called Turnaround: Arts, which also involves a shared public/private effort to keep the arts strong in public education.

It has been a great experiment in bringing together public institutions, such as city government and the U.S. Department of

Education, to partner with private contributors. In the end this enabled us to accomplish far more than we would have if we chose to just rely on either public or private funding exclusively.

Throughout my career, I have been truly honored to help support a host of charities, among them St. Jude Children's Hospitals; the American Cancer Society, for which for the last sixteen years I've created a holiday card to raise money for the cause; and the Juvenile Diabetes Research Foundation. I am proud of the entertainment community, which has done so much to help out others in need, including the Elton John AIDS Foundation, and Sting and his wife Trudie Styler's Rainforest Foundation. I was thrilled to learn from Lady Gaga about her creation of the Born This Way Foundation. It was particularly meaningful for me to be able to help out from the outset with the establishment of the Amy Winehouse Foundation, started by Mitch and Jane Winehouse in memory of their beautiful daughter. When you give back, you get back—and along the way, you find that the return from giving of yourself to others is the greatest gift of all.

Here are websites for the charities that I feel most passionately about, in case you want to learn more or make a donation:

Exploring the Arts: www.exploringthearts.org

American Cancer Society: www.cancer.org

St. Jude Children's Hospital: www.stjude.org

Juvenile Diabetes Research Foundation: www.jdrf.org

Amy Winehouse Foundation: www.amywinehousefoundation.org

Born This Way Foundation: www.bornthiswayfoundation.org

Elton John AIDS Foundation: http://ejaf.org

Rainforest Foundation: www.rainforestfoundation.org

Help USA: www.helpusa.org

Clinton Global Initiative: www.clintonglobalinitiative.org

The Zen of Bennett

The arts are important for education, and for the morale of the entire country.

Students with high arts involvement watch less television, do better in school, participate in more community service activities, and have higher graduation rates—so it's so important for kids to be involved in the arts.

Giving back is one of the best things that anyone can do.

Jon Burr

22

This Too Shall Pass

As wonderful as being in the entertainment world can be, the trials and tribulations of becoming successful and working endless hours can take their toll on a person. It all seems so glamorous, but there is a lot of waiting around. I recall a time when I appeared with Sinatra, and the two of us were escorted down the service elevator and through the back corridors of the hotel ballroom where we were performing. Just as we approached the doors to the stage, Frank turned to me and said, "Hey, Tone, do you realize how many kitchens we've walked through?" We both just looked at each other and chuckled. So it's not all wine and roses.

I'm not complaining, mind you; it comes with the territory. But sometimes the general public doesn't understand this. Trying to do the important things, like maintaining a semblance of family life can become quite a challenge; the travel alone can keep you from doing that.

But even in the lowest moments of my life, I've always felt, *This too shall pass, and then things will get better.* The first devastating event in my life was the death of my father. My dad was a warm, sensitive man, full of love for his family. I can still vividly recall looking into his dark, expressive eyes as I fell asleep while cradled in his strong arms.

Soon after my older brother, John, was born, my father became ill. By the time I was one, my dad's health prevented him from being able to work at all. Doctors said he had a weak heart as a result of having rheumatic fever as a child, but they couldn't help him back then. His body started to ache so badly at night that he couldn't stand having the covers touching his skin. My father would become so congested that he couldn't breathe, and he went in and out of the hospital on Governors Island, often being taken there in the middle of the night. To a young child, this was incredibly confusing. One night when he had an attack, my mother began to panic. Everyone was running around, and he was taken to the hospital again. There he contracted pneumonia on top of congestive heart failure, and he fell semiconscious.

I visited him in the hospital every day, holding his hand tightly and praying that he would recover. After several days he seemed better, and the doctors said he'd be able to come home with us soon. The next morning we got his bedroom ready and went to the hospital to bring him home. The doctor came out to the waiting room, and to our complete shock, told us that my father had died in the night.

We were just so heartbroken; I couldn't believe he was gone. That evening the whole family came to the apartment, and in her despair, a family member told John and me that we had killed our father. I was horrified; I had just lost my dad, and now I had been told it was my fault. I don't think my mother even knew this had been said to us. The awful idea that I had killed my father was planted in my mind, and this caused me extreme pain for quite a while afterward.

After Dad's funeral, my uncle Dominick decided to bring me to live with him and his wife in Pyrites, a small town in upstate New York, so my mother would have one less child to look after. I assumed my mom would never go for this, but in her anguish, she agreed, and I was sent away with them.

My uncle and aunt probably meant well, but they didn't have children of their own and they didn't know how to deal with a child. They owned a grocery store and also farmed, and since it was summer and I wasn't in school, I spent the day helping out with the chores. One day my aunt asked me to sing to her while she was preparing food in the kitchen, so I began singing. My uncle came in and yelled at me for not working, and after that, he made me sleep on the floor.

I was miserable there and missed my family something awful. I stayed in Pyrites for the whole school year before I got to return to my mom and siblings, and, boy, was I glad to get back home. They had moved to a smaller apartment, and my mother was still working all day long and bringing extra sewing home at night, but at least I was in familiar surroundings again with people who loved me.

Somehow I got through that period. And when I look back on it, I realize that the lesson I learned through it all was how to cope with loneliness. I used that skill throughout my life. Although I love traveling around the world, most people don't realize how lonely it can be out there. I learned how to deal with "the blues" for the first time upstate, in Pyrites.

Christmas of 1965 was another extremely low point in my life. My career was thriving, but my marriage of thirteen years to Patricia, the mother of my two boys, was falling apart. We were separated, and I spent Christmas and New Year's in a lonely hotel room in New York City. I was absolutely miserable about not being able to see my sons.

I was all alone in my hotel room, feeling very blue. Suddenly I heard glorious music. I got out of bed and checked the television to see if I'd left it on, but it was turned off. Then I realized that the noise was emanating from the hallway. I opened the door, and standing there was an entire choir, singing "On a Clear Day, You Can See Forever." It's a moment I will never forget.

Duke Ellington was giving a sacred music concert at the Fifth Avenue Presbyterian Church, but I hadn't been able to muster the energy to go to it. My friend Louis Bellson had told Duke that I was feeling down, and he'd sent the choir over to cheer me up. It was one of the most moving gifts I've ever received. That night was as bad as it gets, but this wonderful gesture revived my spirits, no matter how hard things were for me at that moment.

This period of my life was particularly challenging. Trouble really started to brew for me and my recording career in 1966, when the new head of Columbia Records, former lawyer Clive Davis, became president of the label. As I mentioned earlier, he began to make all of the artists, no matter what their background, do rock and roll songs. It was a difficult time for all of the traditional singers, and by 1967, I realized that the company was not looking after my best interests.

Clive sat me down and told me that the only way he'd promote me was if I would record some contemporary music. I didn't have a problem doing songs that were hits, as long as they were good ones and I could interpret them my way. But Clive wasn't content with that, and our standoff continued. I asked Count Basie what he thought I should do. Basie told me in his wise way, "Why change an apple?" So I stuck with what made sense for me.

By 1968, it seemed everything was going down the drain. My divorce was still dragging on. My mother had become very ill. Whenever I went to visit her, I thought it might be the last time I'd ever see her. Then, too, there was the ongoing dispute with Columbia Records.

Finally I caved under the pressure from Davis and agreed to do an album called *Tony Sings the Great Hits of Today.* That's when I literally regurgitated before the first recording session, I was so upset about it. Davis pushed the album so that it sold well, and of course then he wanted me to do another, but I couldn't go through with it.

One day after an argument with Clive and his buddies, on my way out of the office I heard one of them say, "We have to get rid of that wop!" That was the final blow; I told them I wanted out. After long negotiations, we agreed that I'd give them two more records, produced by myself, and then I would be free. After twenty-two years, I decided to take a break from Columbia Records. I knew I had to pick myself up and get ready to start all over again.

It was during these years that Lena Horne and I went on tour together, and she was a great inspiration to me. She had recently lost three important men in her life—her father, her son, and also her husband of twenty years. But even after enduring that, she was the most professional artist I'd ever worked with. She always gave her all, even when she was just rehearsing. I was very impressed with her grit. By example, she taught me a lot about discipline and simply carrying on, even when you don't think you'll get your head above water.

One of the very worst events of my entire life was Thanksgiving night, 1977, when I found out that my mother had died. I was just about to go onstage at the Fairmont Hotel in San Francisco when I heard the news. I just burst through the door of the hotel and when I got outside, I ran for miles. My mom had been the one person in my life who kept me grounded. I thought I would never get over her death.

On top of my grief over my mother, my second wife, Sandra, and I were not getting along at all. And for the first time ever, I wasn't signed with a record label. I had started an independent record company, Improv Records, but it had folded earlier that year, and it was badly in debt. I had fallen behind in my taxes, and the IRS wanted payment. I began to experience severe bouts of depression.

One night I overindulged in drugs and passed out in the bathtub. I could have died, and after that, I realized I had to get my life in order. I recalled the great business advice that my son Danny had always given me, and asked if he and my other son, Dae, would want to come to the West Coast to help me figure things out. They agreed, and arrived the next day.

I told them what was happening, and they said they would look into things. Back in New York, they met with my accountant, and Danny organized all the facts and figures. As I described earlier, he explained to me that I was spending too much, both on the road and personally. He worked out a plan to pay back the IRS, and a new budget for us to stick to. Soon thereafter Sandra and I separated. I moved back to Manhattan, got a one-bedroom apartment, and lived much more frugally than before.

From such a low point, Danny helped me reinvigorate my career. When I look back, even though I struggled to keep my integrity, it has really paid off to stick to my guns. Believe me when I say I'm speaking from experience that you can recover from even the bleakest moments in your life if you simply persevere and believe that you can.

The Zen of Bennett

This too shall pass. Even in the lowest times, realize that things will get better.

The difficult times make you stronger. From failure you can correct yourself and become a better human being.

You can recover from even the bleakest moments if you simply persevere and believe that you can.

Ronnie White

23

I Sing to the Whole Family

I do not like the whole notion of demographics. As a performer, I play to the whole audience. When I was growing up, the main source of entertainment was the movie houses. For a nickel, you would buy a ticket in the morning and stay all day if you wanted to. That meant that whatever they were showing had to appeal to everybody. They had newsreels, human-interest shorts, cartoons, serials, and then at least two feature movie presentations. Sometimes they even had live performers appear between films. But an act wouldn't go over well if it didn't appeal to the entire family.

That's the only thing that makes sense to me, and it makes for smart business, too. The more people who buy your product, the more money you'll make. When you're an entertainer, you want to reach as many people as possible. By only playing to young people, and forgetting their parents and grandparents, you're eliminating a lot of your audience, on purpose. If something is excellent, it defies demographics. Just consider *The Wizard of Oz*, *Snow White*, or any Fred Astaire–Ginger Rogers film. They still look like they were made yesterday, and undeniably they remain the favorites of all ages.

I think that it was a huge mistake for Alan Freed, the deejay who coined the term *rock and roll*, to invent the whole demographic concept. I don't like the idea that one type of music is for a certain age group and no one else, and that your parents have to like another kind of music. Who came up with that? When you're an entertainer, you want to reach as many people as possible. I love performing in a concert hall where I see all the generations coming to hear my music, and where no one needs to be left out.

When I did a date in Palm Beach, Florida, at Donald Trump's Mar-a-Lago Club, which has an older audience, I announced, "If anyone has to go to the bathroom in the middle of the show, I'll understand." But the very next night at the Broward Center for the Performing Arts, also in Florida, every seat was packed with people of all ages. Look at classical music; when you listen to Bach, you think, *That's incredible. How could anybody be that great?* It's not dated in the least. If music sounds dated, that means it wasn't very good in the first place. If something is really good, it's always going to be good; it doesn't change according to who's listening to it.

The whole industry's doing demographics, and that's why

they're going bankrupt—but I'm anti-demographic. The television and newspaper people think demographically when they want to attract an audience, but their most successful shows and publications are the ones that the whole family enjoys. It's simple math, but they never seem to learn the lesson.

Mitch Miller always wanted to put me into a commercial box. My passion was for jazz, but they positioned me as a traditional pop singer because I'm white, which isn't the preconceived idea of what a jazz artist should be. Yet the music that I made with the giants of jazz, such as Stan Getz and Bill Evans, are still the best records in my collection.

It was the jazz singer Annie Ross who made the suggestion to Bill Evans and me that we record together. And as I've said, of all the recordings I've ever made, this one is considered the most prestigious, with the highest-level musicians. I did a television show a while ago with the London Symphony, and on the first break of rehearsal, a few of the classical musicians came up to me with that album for me to sign. It was such an honor that these great musicians had chosen this album out of all of my records for me to autograph.

Back in the sixties, I was told I had to change my music for the kids to accept me. Yet through the years, every age responds to my singing, even though I haven't changed a thing; I just continue to be myself. Kids today are like those from any era: they're open-minded and excited. And they don't want to be put into a box about their music or books or films, any more than I do—they want to enjoy what they like, and to be free to choose. Each new generation of young people has accepted me into their hearts and lives, which is incredibly gratifying.

My recording of "The Way You Look Tonight" connected me to many of the kids. During the red carpet and wrap-up for the Academy Awards one year, they used my version of the song the whole time. As a result, I still have college students coming up to me and saying, "Could you sing 'The Way You Look Tonight'?" Young people are very smart; if they're given something hip, they'll respond to it.

Louis Armstrong created one of the most enduring styles of music when he invented swing. When you have that in your bones, there's nothing like it. There's a whole army of Americans who love swing when they hear it. Their parents danced to it for years and years, and they grew up hearing these songs. And if you combine a swing tune with great lyrics, then you've got yourself a hit. When Duke said, "Sing sweet, but put a little dirt in it," that's what he was talking about. Always make it swing. Then when you add a well-crafted lyric, you also become a master storyteller, and your work will last for a hundred years.

It's fortunate that today there's a whole group of younger artists who play on a more mature level, like Diana Krall and Michael Bublé. These musicians are really communicating with the public, and they are enjoying success because they're playing to the entire family. Time is a great leveler; you can be assured that the cream will always rise to the top.

The Zen of Bennett

If something is excellent, it defies demographics and categorization.

If music can be dated, it wasn't very good in the first place.

Young people don't want to be put into a box about their music or books or films—they want to be free to choose what they like.

"I REMEMBER CLIFFORD"

Clifford Brown

24

I Never Worked a Day in My Life

I feel that I have so much more to learn. Here I am at eighty-six, and it's like starting all over again when I look at the knowledge that I'd like to acquire. I'm studying more now than I've ever studied in my life—and I have at least another ten to fifteen years before I accomplish what I want to.

I like challenges; I don't want to be put on a shelf. I never think, *Okay, I've done it all, so let me just retire.* I could have done that twenty years ago. But work eliminates my headaches—it's what keeps me sane. When you are constantly studying and expanding your mind, you're never really finished. No matter what level you reach, there's always the next level to aspire to.

As a young person, I realized that education was the way to go. My sister, Mary, who was a librarian, instilled that in me, so I became a perpetual student. I've just recently taken up sculpting. It's like starting all over; it's not like painting or photography. You have to learn the anatomy of the shoulder, the muscles, how they're all connected and how they're made. Studying anatomy makes you realize what a monument the human body is. So many people are unhappy with themselves physically, but when you realize what you're walking around with anatomically, and that everyone has a different physique that makes them an individual, you learn to appreciate yours a lot more.

I am also always reading, which is the most wonderful thing anyone can do, because you constantly learn from the masters that way. When I first met the poet Allen Ginsberg, we became fast friends after we found out that we shared a love for William Blake. We spent hours just talking about his poems and the imagery he painted with words. I've connected with many people over books, all across the world.

You can't plan life; life plans you. If you stay flexible and roll with it, you can survive. As the great cellist Pablo Casals told me, "At any given moment, you can learn." Isn't that wonderful? And on his deathbed, when Leonardo da Vinci said, "Does anybody ever finish anything?" he realized that there was a lot he still didn't know. This coming from a man who is famous for his artistic and scientific genius.

Michelangelo also understood the concept of lifelong study. He started to paint the ceiling in the Sistine Chapel when he was thirty-three. He would set himself on top of the scaffolding, lying on his back with a candle mounted on his head so he could see in order to complete his masterpiece. Then he went back to paint the Last Judgment on the wall nearly thirty years later, at the age of sixty-one. After he finished what was probably his greatest achievement, he said, "I'm still learning."

I've met artists who are so talented that it makes me shiver. They know so much, and being in their presence makes me realize how much I have yet to achieve. It keeps me even more committed to learning; to honing my performance. Aretha Franklin recently told me that she's taking classical music lessons at Juilliard, which proves that the greats understand the importance of perpetual education and growth.

When the magnificent Japanese painter Hokusai was in his seventies, he said that he was just learning how to paint. That's what I'm trying to do—I'm still looking to grow. Growth takes time. You start by figuring out your motivation—why you want to paint or sing, or do anything in life. And then you hone in on what you're seeking and attempt to become skilled at what that is. Then you find ways to push the envelope further and challenge yourself.

My son and manager Danny, who has managed me for over thirty years now, came to me one day wanting me to try something new. "Why don't you write a song?" he asked. "Well, I can't compete with Cole Porter or Jerome Kern, you know; give me a break," was my reply. But he wouldn't let me off the hook so easily. "Why don't you just try it?" he encouraged me. "We have something in mind."

At first I felt skeptical about it, but then I received my inspiration. After I played a concert in Hawaii, I went to hear a wonderful jazz group perform. One of their songs in particular spoke to me. When I asked the piano player for its name, he told me it was called "Dark Eyes," and was written by Django Reinhardt.

Reinhardt was the great musician and guitarist from Paris who played with Louis Armstrong. In fact, Willie Nelson recently told me that Reinhardt was his favorite guitar player of all time. When Willie was looking for a guitar, he wanted one with a similar sound to Reinhardt's that he could play either onstage or in his hotel room. When he finally found the perfect guitar—which he named Trigger, by the way—he said that Django would have loved the instrument, and I had to agree. So when this pianist in Hawaii told me that this tune was by Reinhardt, it all seemed to come full circle.

I asked Danny to get hold of the family that owned the song, and they gave us an okay for me to write the lyrics, inspired by and dedicated to my wife, Susan Benedetto, which became "All for You." And oddly enough, I wrote the lyrics in only an hour. I guess from interpreting songs for so many years, I know to stay away from trite material, and I thought it came out pretty well. Then when we were in Fresno, California, I performed it in front of an audience for the first time, and I was bowled over by their reaction; they went crazy for it. So at eighty-six, I now have my first songwriting credit.

Some singers' voices start to wobble when they get older. I once asked Sinatra what he'd do to beat wobbling, and he said he wasn't sure, but that if it ever started to happen to his voice, he'd just quit. To avoid that, I work every day doing my scales, and I really concentrate on holding my notes without vibrato. A dear friend and accomplished musician, Abe Katz, who was the first trumpet for the New York Philharmonic, told me that he holds notes with no vibrato, as that's the best way to keep focused so the notes remain strong and clear. And that works for singing, too. If my voice does start to falter at some point, I guess I'll just become a painter.

The late jazz vocalist Joe Williams told me, "It's not that you want to sing; it's that you *have* to sing." And that is true—I have to do it. I can't think of a nobler occupation than to try to make people forget their problems for an hour and a half. You lift up their spirits and give them a feeling of hope. That's what a good psychiatrist does to help patients.

On the day of a show, I can't wait to hit the stage. I prepare all day long to go out there, and I try to get right into the pocket of the public so they have a really great evening. I can't think of a better way to live. I'm never tired of it; every night feels like a new experience, and I've never been bored a single moment when I'm performing.

I have no desire whatsoever to retire; if I'm lucky, I just want to get better as I get older. Through the years, you shed the idea of competition and the desire to be the best; instead, you just want to get better for yourself. And if you do what you're passionate about, the material things will come. I never need a vacation because I have a passion to sing and paint, and I get to do both every day. As far as I'm concerned, I've never worked a day in my life.

I encourage everyone to find their passion. Work as hard as you can to follow your dreams; they will ultimately lead you to contentment in every aspect of your life. It is my goal at the end of each day to be able to lay my head on my pillow, knowing I've tried my best.

There are a lot of things I want to do. I'm blessed with the fact that I have my health, and my wish is for this to continue, so I can keep plugging away for a long time. Long ago, I realized that nobody beats death. You're as good as your last breath. Duke Ellington said it best: "Number one: Don't quit. Number two: Listen to number one."

The Zen of Bennett

It's good to accept challenges. Never let people put you in a box.

You can't plan life; life plans you.

If you stay flexible and roll with the punches, you can survive.

The more you study, the more you learn what to leave out and what to keep in.

A lifelong habit of reading allows you to learn from the masters.

Shed the idea of competition, and of being the best. Instead, desire to improve only by being yourself.

If you follow your passion, you'll never work a day in your life.

Untitled

Acknowledgments

I would like to acknowledge:

My son and manager, Danny Bennett, and the entire RPM Productions team: Sylvia Weiner, Hadley Spanier, Dawn Olejar, Joe Rhoades, and my assistant, Seth Ferris, for all their support and help at every turn.

I'd like to thank my tour manager, Vance Anderson; my sound man, Tom Young; and my quartet: Lee Musiker, Gray Sargent, Harold Jones, and Marshall Wood; as well as all the musicians who have supported me through the years.

Dick Golden, for his invaluable contributions.

WME and my literary agent, Mel Berger.

HarperCollins, for all their enthusiasm and belief in the project; particularly Lisa Sharkey and Amy Bendell.

Leslie Wells and Jonathan Ehrlich for all their great work.

My wife, Susan Benedetto, for keeping everything on track.

And my dear friend Mitch Albom for his kind words.

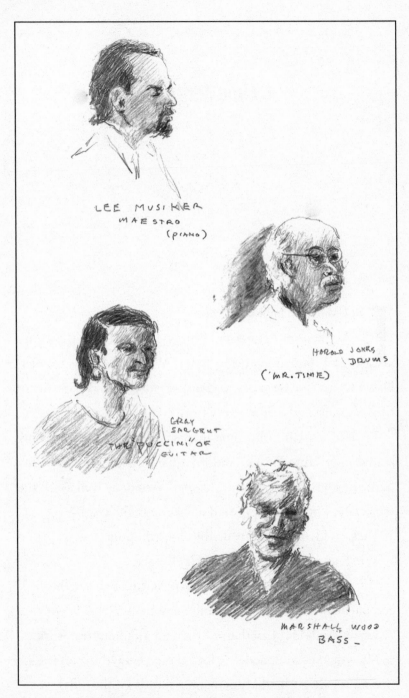

My Quartet: Lee, Harold, Gray, and Marshall

Artwork

Artwork

Self-Portrait

About the Author

Tony Bennett, a true "Renaissance man," grew up in Astoria, Queens, during the Great Depression in a family of Italian immigrants. After serving as an infantryman in World War II, he studied singing, and then signed with Columbia Records, releasing his first hit in 1951. He entered his seventh decade as a recording artist with seventeen Grammy Awards to his name, including the Grammy Lifetime Achievement Award and a multiple Emmy winner. He made history in the 1990s when he won the coveted Grammy Album of the Year for his *MTV Unplugged*, beloved by audiences from nine to ninety. He is credited with heralding in the iPod generation; as the *New York Times* aptly put it, "he has not just bridged the generation gap; he has demolished it." He has performed for eleven United States presidents, and has appeared at seven Royal Command Performances.

About the Author

In addition to performing, Tony Bennett is an accomplished visual artist, with three of his original paintings featured in the permanent collection at the Smithsonian Institution. Tony marched alongside Dr. Martin Luther King in 1965 on the historic march to Selma, and his humanitarian efforts are renowned; the United Nations honored him with their Humanitarian Award in 2007. Bennett founded, in association with the Board of Education in New York City, the Frank Sinatra School of the Arts—a public high school for the arts in his hometown of Astoria, Queens. With his wife, Susan, he established Exploring the Arts, a charitable organization that supports arts education in public high schools in New York City.

Tony is the author of three books, *The Good Life*, *Tony Bennett: What My Heart Has Seen*, and *Tony Bennett in the Studio: A Life of Art and Music*. A new documentary, *The Zen of Bennett*, created and conceived by the singer's son Danny Bennett, recently premiered at the 2012 Tribeca Film Festival, and is a companion project to this latest book by Tony, *Life Is a Gift: The Zen of Bennett*.

Tony Bennett's timeless appeal has endured, and will continue to do so—for his passion, dedication, and joy for his artistry does not diminish, and in fact continues to grow and inspire his many generations of fans.